# LET THEM ANOINT THE SICK

# Let Them Anoint the Sick

JOHN J. ZIEGLER

THE LITURGICAL PRESS
Collegeville, Minnesota

THE LITURGICAL PRESS
Collegeville, Minnesota 56321

Cover design by Ann Blattner.

*Nihil obstat:* Rev. Robert C. Harren, J.C.L., *Censor deputatus.*
*Imprimatur:* ✛ George H. Speltz, Apostolic Administrator, Diocese of St. Cloud.
April 9, 1987.

Copyright © 1987 by The Order of St. Benedict, Inc., Collegeville, Minnesota. No part of this book may be reproduced in any form or by any means without the written permission of the publisher except for brief quotations embodied in critical articles or reviews.

Manufactured in the United States of America.

---

**Library of Congress Cataloging-in-Publication Data**
Ziegler, John J. (John Joseph), 1939–
  Let them anoint the sick.
  Bibliography: p.
  Includes index.
  1. Unction—History.  2. Deacons—Catholic Church.
3. Laity—Catholic Church.  4. Catholic Church—
Doctrines.  I. Title.
BX2203.Z54  1987         265'.7         87-3054
ISBN 0-8146-1553-8 (pbk.)

I would like to express my gratitude to my parents, family, and friends who encouraged and supported me in the research that led to this study. I am especially grateful to Sharon Cirincione, Mickey Dalton, Bob Hennigan, and Mike Meagher, who assisted me in the preparation of the manuscript.

This work is respectfully and lovingly dedicated to all those who have touched my life deeply and have convinced me that it is only by faith—that belief in oneself, in the love of those around us, and above all in the abiding presence of our loving God—that the experience of pain can be transformed into fulfillment, peace, and joy.

JOHN J. ZIEGLER

# CONTENTS

| | | |
|---|---|---:|
| ABBREVIATIONS | | viii |
| INTRODUCTION | | 1 |
| 1 | *Theological Presuppositions* | 7 |
| 2 | *The Anointing of the Sick in the First Four Centuries* | 26 |
| 3 | *The Anointing of the Sick from Innocent I to the Carolingian Reform* | 41 |
| 4 | *The Anointing of the Sick from the Carolingian Reform to the Middle Ages* | 58 |
| 5 | *The Anointing of the Sick from the Middle Ages to the Sixteenth Century* | 71 |
| 6 | *The Teaching of the Protestant Reformers on the Sacrament of Extreme Unction* | 88 |
| 7 | *The Response of the Pre-Tridentine Catholic Apologists* | 103 |
| 8 | *The Response of the Council of Trent* | 111 |
| 9 | *Let Them Anoint the Sick* | 144 |
| NOTES | | 155 |
| BIBLIOGRAPHY | | 179 |

# ABBREVIATIONS

CT     *Concilium Tridentinum: Diariorum, actorum, epistolarum, tractatuum nova collectio* (Freiburg i. Br., 1901ff.).

DS     H. Denzinger, *Enchiridion symbolorum definitionum et declarationum de rebus fidei et morum*, 33rd ed. by A. Schönmetzer (Freiburg i. Br., 1965).

DTC     *Dictionnaire de théologie catholique*, 16 vols. (Paris, 1903-65).

Mansi     J. D. Mansi, ed., *Sacrorum conciliorum nova et amplissima collectio*, 31 vols. (Florence, 1759-98; reprinted and continued, Paris, Leipzig, and Arnheim, 1901-27).

PG     J. P. Migne, ed., *Patrologia Graeca*, 161 vols. (Paris, 1857-66).

PL     J. P. Migne, ed., *Patrologia Latina*, 221 vols. (Paris, 1844-64).

# INTRODUCTION

This study addresses the question of whether the Church can appoint extraordinary ministers of the sacrament of the anointing of the sick. Since 1551, when the Council of Trent condemned the Reformation teaching that rejected the Church's limiting the administration of this sacrament to priests, it has been accepted as a defined doctrine of the Church that only the priest is the proper minister of anointing. Thus it would appear that this is a closed question.

With the recent restoration of the permanent diaconate to a proper and permanent rank among the hierarchical offices of ministry and the subsequent delineation of the functions and responsibilities of this office, including the deacon's traditional ministry to the sick, this question has taken on renewed significance. In 1973, at the request of a member of the American hierarchy, the American Bishops' Committee on the Permanent Diaconate submitted to the Sacred Congregation for the Sacraments and Divine Worship a petition that the faculty for anointing the sick be given to deacons. The response was strongly in the negative.

Later that year Fr. Paul Palmer, S.J., a respected American sacramental theologian, submitted to the Bishops' Committee on the Permanent Diaconate a paper entitled "Regarding the Deacon as Minister of Anointing of the Sick." In this study Father Palmer provided background information on the question and concluded that "perhaps the time has come to respond more fully to the sacramental needs of the sick and elderly who cannot come to the church by appointing special ministers of the sacrament of the sick."[1]

In response to this position, Msgr. Joseph Baker, personal theologian to the Cardinal-Archbishop of St. Louis, prepared a report entitled "On the Minister of the Sacrament of the Anointing of the Sick," in which he objected to Father Palmer's conclusion, citing as his reason canon 4 of the Council of Trent, which states:

> If anyone says that the presbyters of the Church whom blessed James exhorts to be brought in to anoint the sick are not the priests ordained by a bishop but the elders by age in each community, and that for this reason the priest alone is not the proper minister of extreme unction, A.S. (DS 1719).

In 1975 the Bishops' Committee on the Permanent Diaconate requested that this author develop a study that would address specifically the impact of the Tridentine teaching on this particular question. As a result of extensive research both into the history of the sacrament and the deliberations of the Council of Trent, it was his conclusion that the teaching of Trent on the proper minister of extreme unction need not be considered an obstacle to the Church's appointment of someone other than the priest as a minister of the sacramental anointing of the sick.

Copies of these papers were sent to all the members of the American hierarchy as well as to the Vatican Secretariat of State and the Sacred Congregations for the Doctrine of the Faith and for the Sacraments and Divine Worship. Despite continued petitions from permanent diaconate offices of various national conferences of bishops, the Holy See, when it promulgated the new *Pastoral Care of the Sick: Rites of Anointing and Viaticum* in 1982, upheld the present practice of the Church.[2]

In the meantime a new phenomenon has arisen with regard to the pastoral care of the sick, especially in North America. More and more, Catholic patients of many hospitals, nursing homes, and other health care facilities are being cared for by pastoral teams that frequently are comprised of deacons, non-ordained religious, and officially commissioned lay ministers, the majority of whom have been competently trained and certified to care pastorally for the sick. In some instances a priest-chaplain assigned to an institution serves as a member of these teams. Where this is not the case, however, priests who are charged with other primary pastoral responsibilities have to be summoned to administer the sacrament of anointing when necessary.

Since the members of these pastoral teams are the ones who have direct daily contact with the patients and their families, who console and respond to the needs of the infirm in their moment of crisis, who assure them of the prayers and support of the broader community of faith, it is clear that the presence and concern of the Church at large are made visible and tangible through their ministry. Consequently, it has been observed that pastorally it is often awkward when a priest who is a total stranger or who has had little contact with the patient celebrates this sacrament which epitomizes the Church's total pastoral concern for the sick person.

In other words, if the patient is judged to be comfortable with having the sacrament administered by someone other than the priest, would it not be more appropriate pastorally for a member of the team that has already established a personal relationship with the patient to celebrate the sacrament, regardless of whether or not he or she has been ordained to any of the hierarchical offices of ministry? If an officially appointed member of a particular healthcare team were to administer the sacrament of anointing, not only would it be clear that he or she is acting publicly in the name of the Church, but also such an administration would communicate more effectively to the sick person the love and faith of the entire Church and the saving presence of Christ. Thus, in light of the Church's commitment to a more developed and total pastoral care of the sick, and of the recently restored understanding of the meaning and practice of the sacrament of anointing, it is of great pastoral, liturgical, and theological importance that the question of whether the Church can appoint someone other than the ordained priest to administer this sacrament be reopened.

It should be recognized from the outset that this question is complex and that there are several other issues related to it. One such issue involves the relationship between the sacraments of anointing and reconciliation. Even though there has been considerable debate down through the centuries regarding what sins are forgiven by this anointing and how this is achieved, traditionally the spiritual effects of the sacrament have always included the forgiveness of sins. When the anointing of the sick became one of the "last sacraments," the normal practice was to administer it together with the sacrament of penance and Viaticum. The commonly held teaching that only a priest can administer the sacrament of penance further solidified the position that only the priest is the proper minister of anointing.

Since the Second Vatican Council, the sacrament of anointing has been restored to a significance and use proper to itself. While the renewed rite includes the opportunity for the celebration of reconciliation, that is not always required. Even in its restored sense, sacramental anointing is not to be understood as a substitute for confession. It is recognized, however, that with the contrition of the recipient and, if necessary, a promise to receive sacramental absolution at a later time, the sacrament of the sick does remit sins. Therefore, whether anyone other than the priest can administer the sacrament of penance, while a related topic, remains a distinct question.

A second related issue has to do with the difference between ordination to a hierarchical office of ministry and the official commissioning and assignment of lay ministers to a particular function of ministry. This involves the question of whether there is communicated with ordination a power to administer sacraments that is not included in an official commissioning. This power would be of such a nature that, at least in the case of the sacrament of the anointing of the sick, there would be no sacrament without it.

This study will not discuss in great depth either of these two related issues. Instead, it will focus its attention on the Tridentine canon that has traditionally been cited as preventing the Church from appointing anyone other than an ordained priest to anoint the sick.

Until recently, past formulations of doctrine, including the canons of Trent, have frequently been used in a highly uncritical fashion both in theological manuals and by the authorities of the Church. Because these documents are historical, they need to be examined in the light of their historical setting, and only then can they be accurately interpreted as to what degree they are to determine questions and practices of a later period.

By way of a remote historical context for the Tridentine teaching on extreme unction, this study will trace the development of the Church's understanding and practice of the anointing of the sick from the time of the New Testament to the time prior to the Reformation. Special attention will be focused on the following questions: How have commentators interpreted the two principal scriptural texts associated with the sacrament? How have historical writers understood the letter of Pope Innocent I to Decentius, which is traditionally accepted as being the earliest important nonbiblical document that indisputably refers to the sacramental anointing of the sick? Has there been any development in the consciousness of the Church with regard to anointing as a sacrament? Finally, in what ways did this sacrament undergo modifications in its external form or mode of administration in the centuries prior to Trent?

This remote context will be indispensable for evaluating the degree of thoroughness with which Trent formulated its teaching on extreme unction, and it will also present a vantage point from which the historical accuracy of the deliberations of the Council regarding this sacrament can be evaluated. Such an evaluation will contribute to the discovery of the precise intention and meaning of the Council's teaching on the sacrament in general and on its proper minister in particular.

The more immediate historical context of the Council's deliberations on this sacrament is the teaching of the Reformers on sacramental institution and the minister of the sacraments. The Tridentine responses in canons 1 and 10 of Session 7 on *De sacramentis in genere* deal, respectively, with the institution and number of the sacraments and the question of who is empowered to administer the sacraments.[3] As a corollary to Trent's teaching on the institution of the sacraments, the Council's discussion leading to the promulgation of the canons in Session 21 on the reception of Communion under both species gives an invaluable insight into the mind of the Council on the specific competency of the Church to make changes regarding the sacraments.[4]

Finally, the actual context for canon 4 is the teaching of the Reformers on the sacrament of anointing and their specific position regarding the minister of extreme unction. A detailed investigation and analysis of the discussions and decisions of the theologians and the Council Fathers from which the specific canons promulgated by Trent on this sacrament were formulated will identify both the accuracy of the Council's understanding of the Reformers' teaching on extreme unction and the degree of familiarity the Council Fathers had regarding the historical development of the understanding and practice of the Church's sacramental anointing of the sick. The origin and evolution of the specific canon on the proper minister of anointing will be traced, and there will be a careful scrutiny for any signs that might clearly explicate in what sense the Council promulgated this canon as "heretical" and deserving of condemnation by anathema.

On the basis of this examination of the Tridentine deliberations, a number of observations and conclusions will be drawn that will substantiate the conclusion of this author that canon 4 of Session 14 need no longer be considered an obstacle to the Church's appointment of someone other than an ordained priest as an extraordinary minister of the sacrament of the anointing of the sick.

*Chapter One*

# THEOLOGICAL PRESUPPOSITIONS

Before developing the remote historical context for the Tridentine teaching on the proper minister of the sacramental anointing of the sick, it is necessary to identify several presuppositions drawn from contemporary theological scholarship which legitimize the posing of the question of whether the Church can appoint someone other than the priest to administer the sacrament of the sick. These presuppositions include the insights of modern sacramental theology concerning the competence of the Church regarding the sacraments, the conclusions of recent investigations into early Church order, and the work of a number of theologians who have begun to apply various methods of critical interpretation to certain canons of the Council of Trent.

## The Competence of the Church in Sacramental Matters

The very question of whether the Church can appoint extraordinary ministers of anointing presupposes that in fact the Church has the authority to institute change in at least some areas of sacramental administration. Even a cursory historical survey of the sacraments demonstrates that through the centuries many of the sacraments have undergone considerable ecclesiastical modification. Theologians have always recognized this competence of the Church, but they have not always agreed on the extent to which the Church can modify the celebration and administration of each of the sacraments.

The extent of the Church's power over the sacraments is traditionally considered in conjunction with the theological teaching on sacramental institution. Because of their nature as grace-giving events of the New Law, the sacraments have always been considered to be of divine origin and not the mere product of human or ecclesiastical invention. The problem centers around the manner in which the sacraments were instituted by the Lord and what is considered to be of divine determination, and therefore immutable, as distinct from what is ecclesiastical in origin.

Recognizing that the sacraments give grace and forgive sins, the Scholastic theologians were in agreement that each of the sacraments in some way looks to Christ as its author. However, in the case of several of the sacraments, given the absence in the Scriptures of any clear reference to their being instituted by the Lord as well as the fact that historically these sacraments have undergone development even in some of their essential elements, there was disagreement over the extent of Christ's determination in their regard.

According to the Thomists, Christ directly instituted all the sacraments and determined the essential aspects of each one of them, even though the Scriptures frequently are silent about much of this.[1] Aquinas explained this silence by the general claim that not all things are found in the Scriptures and by stating that the New Testament notes Christ's promulgation of only those sacraments that were more difficult to believe. Thus, according to Thomas, it was left to the Apostles to promulgate the others such as confirmation and extreme unction (*Summa* III, 29, a. 3).

The Franciscans, on the other hand, especially Alexander of Hales and Bonaventure, were more sensitive to the silence of the Scriptures and the fact of historical development. While admitting that all the sacraments trace their origin to the Lord, they did not conclude that each of them was directly instituted by him. They used imprecise terms such as "initiating" or "insinuating" to describe the action of Christ.

The Franciscan theologians recognized the special importance and unique role of the Holy Spirit, the Apostles, and the Church in the further determination of several sacraments, especially confirmation and extreme unction. While they held that whatever was determined later was always on the authority of Christ, these "further determinations" were understood to be more than the mere promulgation of what had already been fixed by the Lord, extending even to the assigning of the matter and form of the sacrament.[2] The Franciscans did not indicate, however, whether they considered these determinations made by the Apostolic Church and even by the post-Apostolic Church to be normative for all time.

Contemporary sacramental theology, especially as developed by Karl Rahner, S.J., and Edward Schillebeeckx, O.P., uses a different approach to explain sacramental institution and the competency of the Church over the sacraments. Beginning with a Christological statement that the acts of Jesus as the human incarnation of the redeeming love of God were in fact divine acts in visible form possessing saving power, theologians today refer to these acts as "sacramental." Consequently, Jesus is seen as the primordial sacrament in and through whom all people are called to salvation.

It is through the Church, the visible realization of the primordial sacrament in time and history, that the human person encounters this saving reality. According to Rahner,

> the Church is the abiding presence of that primordial sacramental word of definite grace which Christ is in the world, effecting what is uttered, by uttering it in sign. By the very fact of being in that way the enduring presence of Christ in the world, the Church is truly the fundamental sacrament.[3]

Regarding those actions which in the strictest sense of the word are traditionally called sacraments, Rahner notes:

> When the Church in her official, organized public capacity precisely as the source of redemptive grace meets the individual in the actual ultimate accomplishment of her nature, there we have the sacraments in the proper sense.[4]

The sacraments, therefore, are those vital acts of the Church whereby there is visibly brought into actualization the very essence of what the Church is: the historically visible manifestation of the continued presence of the redemptive grace of God in the world. Given this notion of sacrament, it is evident that by their very nature they are of divine origin and have been instituted in some way by Christ, even though this institution may only have been generic.

Modern sacramental theology does not see the need to have recourse to a definite statement by the historical Jesus as evidence of his institution of the sacraments. Rahner writes:

> A fundamental act of the Church in an individual's regard, in situations that are decisive for him, an act which truly involves the nature of the Church as the historical, eschatological presence of redemptive grace is *ipso facto* a sacrament, even if it were only later that reflection was directed to its sacramental character that follows from its connection with the nature of the Church. The institution of a sacrament can follow simply from the fact that Christ founded the Church with its sacramental nature.[5]

Significant in this position of Rahner is the role that the consciousness of the Church can play in the recognition of a certain act as being a visible accomplishment of the nature of the Church and therefore sacramental. It would appear that in such a process a sacrament could be identified on the basis of an *a posteriori* experience of these actions as already present and operative. Recognizing its nature in its actual concrete fulfillment, the Church is able to determine that certain activities which it has already carried out spontaneously are in accord with what it is and are essential to its own nature without having to be informed of this explicitly.[6]

Schillebeeckx likewise recognizes the institution of the seven sacraments as being implicit in the establishment of the Church as sacrament. In addition, he is of the opinion that Christ also established the sevenfold direction of grace of which the visible acts of the Church are the medium.[7] He admits that the ways in which Christ may have manifested his will may vary for the different sacraments, and in some cases this manifestation may be difficult to pinpoint with certainty. Furthermore, like Rahner, Schillebeeckx holds that the divine will need not be expressed explicitly. It could be that an implicit but real manifestation of God's will could become more explicit in the later consciousness of the faith in the light of the Church's sacramental practice.

According to Schillebeeckx, the outward shape of some of the sacraments may not have been determined by Christ but left to the Apostolic Church. In such cases, even though this apostolic determination is traditionally accepted as normative for all time, it most likely would have been very rudimentary. Thus, while preserving this apostolic core, there could be a broader development of what might have been rudimentary and undifferentiated. Moreover, he notes that any determination made by the post-Apostolic Church on the basis of its ecclesial authority of jurisdiction, while necessary for the validity of the sacrament at any given time, can change.

> The Church of later times (always in keeping with the socio-religious rules governing amendments to the symbolism of a community) is itself to redetermine the embodiment of its own symbolic sacramental acts, as long as the direction of sacramental meaning instituted by Christ can still be represented by and imaged in the embodiment chosen (which after all is the essence of symbolic activity).[8]

Schillebeeckx suggests that this explains the various historical changes the sacramental rites have undergone.

Neither Rahner nor Schillebeeckx has any difficulty asserting that all the sacraments were directly instituted by Christ, even though in some cases only generically so, and at the same time accepting both the silence of the Scriptures regarding this institution and the historically documented fact of sacramental development. What is of particular importance is the function that the consciousness of the Church plays in the explicit recognition that certain acts are in fact an essential actualization of the Church as the fundamental sacrament, and therefore are sacraments properly speaking.

In the instances of generic institution by Christ, the spontaneous selection by the Apostolic Church of a certain rite or essential aspect in which the Christian significance is sacramentalized is considered to be binding *in perpetuo* and normative. Nevertheless, contemporary sacramental theology recognizes that this selection can be developed by the Church beyond its basic primitive determination. Moreover, these subsequent determinations by the post-Apostolic Church can be modified as long as what is necessary for validity in virtue of the institution of Christ or the apostolic-ecclesial determination is maintained.

Given, therefore, this understanding of the competence of the Church to make changes regarding the sacraments, there arises the following question: Is canon 4 of the Council of Trent on the minister of extreme unction, based as it is on the apostolic instruction of James (5:14-15), an apostolic determination necessary for the valid administration of this sacrament and therefore forever normative?

**Recent Scholarship on Early Church Order**

It would appear from a reading of canon 4 that the Council of Trent identified the "presbyters" in the text from James as priests ordained by a bishop, as though the New Testament use of "presbyter" in general, and that of James in particular, has in all times past been interpreted as "priest." Recent scholarship that has carefully investigated early Church order makes such an assumption somewhat questionable. Because it is important for the purposes of this study to know how the Christian community about and for whom James was writing understood those who were called in to anoint and pray over the sick person, attention must be paid to the findings of those who in recent years have examined the origins of those offices of ministry that were present in the Church at the time of the Council of Trent.

*Church Order in the New Testament*

In New Testament times, the priesthood in Israel had become a somewhat closed caste dedicated principally to the service of the Temple. Resulting from this was a vocabulary which could be termed "priestly" and which was predominantly cultic. The ordinary Hebrew word for "priest" at this time was *kohen*, which the Septuagint translated as *hiereus*. The term was variously applied in the New Testament to Jewish and pagan priests, to Christ, in particular in the Epistle to the Hebrews (10:12-14), and to all members of the Christian community (1 Pet 2:9; Rev 1:6; 5:10; 20:6).

Most scholars see the application of the title to Christ, especially in the period after the destruction of the Temple, as an effort to demonstrate that Christ the priest and his priestly act have replaced the priesthood and sacrifices of Israel. Regarding the priestly designation of all the Christian people, the term appears to be used in a more spiritualized sense. In other words, the Epistle of Peter refers more to "priestly holiness" than to specific priestly cultic functions. Raymond Brown writes:

> The idea of a universal Christian priesthood is never connected in the New Testament in any way with the Eucharist. The statement in I Peter 2:5 that Christians offer "spiritual sacrifices" is a figurative reference to a holy way of life.[9]

What is of significance, however, is the fact that not only does the New Testament purposely avoid referring to any Christian minister as "priest,"[10] but it indicates that in the early Church there was in process a development with regard to both the structure and understanding of the Church's ministry.

It appears from the writings of Paul that the ministry in the Churches founded by him was not well developed. To a great degree this was due not only to the fact that Paul continued to exercise leadership over these communities, even though he himself was continually on the move, but also to the fact that these communities enjoyed a highly charismatic nature. In describing the ministry, Paul seems to mingle both offices and charisms, and frequently it is difficult to draw a clear-cut distinction between the two (1 Cor 12:28; Eph 4:11; Rom 12:6-8). Among these various ministries, Paul gives priority, after the apostles, to the prophets and teachers, whose functions bore a special relation to the Word. Also included among the ministries is the task of administration. It is difficult to determine from Paul's writings exactly what was involved in the exercise of this function.

In the Epistle to the Philippians (1:1), Paul specifically addresses the bishops (*episkopoi*) and deacons (*diakonoi*) of the Church there. The title *episkopos* occurs frequently in profane Greek. Among its various significances, the title was used to refer to an official overseer or guardian, and it can be supposed that the specific appellation *episkopos* here bears reference to the general charism of administration. In this regard, Daniel Donovan observes that the title *episkopos* would not be a new creation but the use of more precise vocabulary.[11]

According to the first chapters of the Acts of the Apostles, the Church at Jerusalem was primarily under the leadership of the Apostles. Later chapters indicate that this leadership role was shared by what might be termed a "Christian sanhedrin" composed of apostles and presbyters.

It is important to note that the Jewish presbyters of New Testament times, although ordained through a laying on of hands, were not of the priestly caste. They formed lay bodies that dealt principally with civil governing, judiciary matters, and duties of the synagogue.

In addition to an administrative function, the presbyters also seem to have enjoyed a certain doctrinal authority (Acts 15:5ff.). Moreover, the evidence of Acts does not seem to contradict the idea that they, like their Jewish counterparts, were not exclusively involved with cultic functions. While Acts 14:23 further notes that Paul and Barnabas traveled throughout the Diaspora and appointed presbyters to govern the local Churches, there is no description of what the function of the presbyters was in these communities. Thus the Acts of the Apostles witnesses to two orders of Church structure: that of Jerusalem with its resident college of elders centered around its president, and that of other communities with local ministers who were dependent upon the leadership of the itinerant Paul or another delegated apostle.

In the Pastoral Letters are found the titles of bishop, presbyter, and deacon. Since both *episkopos* and *presbyteros* are titles that pertain to the office of supervision, scholars have questioned to what extent they are distinct. It is generally accepted that these titles, as used in the Pastorals, are at least partially interchangeable.[12]

Those who reject the authentic Pauline authorship of the Pastorals see in them evidence of a gradual coalescing of two traditions of Church order—that of the Pauline Churches with their *episkopoi* (and *diakonoi*) and that of Jerusalem with its council of elders. Authors such as Hans Küng[13] explain the eventual emergence of the threefold hierarchical office of ministry as the result of a confluence of different, culturally distinct, local titles for the same office, which in time became universal titles for different offices.[14] The process of assimilation as presented by Küng would assume that there were no presbyters in the communities founded by Paul. While it is true, in fact, that no concrete mention of *presbyteroi* is made in the indisputably authentic Pauline letters, the argument propounding the absence of any presbyters in these Churches is basically one founded on silence and should not be overestimated.

Although the evidence remains inconclusive as to whether the Christian use of these two titles originated from two completely distinct cultural backgrounds, what is of significance is the fact that in the Churches of the Pastorals, the resident ministries of the presbyter-bishops appear to be clearly present. This would represent a development from the witness of both the early Jerusalem Church and the original communities founded by Paul. What is even more important is the fact that the titles used for the offices of ministry are non-cultic in origin, and neither of these offices is described as being "priestly." Their function was principally administrative and connected with the ministry of the Word—teaching and the preservation of tradition.

## Church Order According to Non-biblical Documents of the First Three Centuries

There are a number of non-biblical documents that give further evidence of that ministerial development, the origin of which is testified to in the Scriptures, which led to the threefold hierarchical office of priestly ministry in the Church.

In the *First Epistle of Clement of Rome* (d. ca. 94), mention is made of the Church at Corinth being under the leadership of Clement, who was based in Rome, and local officers, who are referred to both as presbyters and *episkopoi*. Although Clement alludes to the functions of the Old Testament priesthood, he seems to take great care to mark the differences between the Levitical priesthood and the ministers of the Church whose task was that of preaching and the pastoral care of the flock. In chapter 44, where a clear analogy is drawn between the Christian leaders and the Judaic priesthood, the emphasis is more on the need for a sense of order than on priestly functions.[15]

According to the *Didache*,[16] the privileged place in the community belonged to the itinerant apostles, teachers, and especially the prophets. The tenth chapter (10:7) indicates that the prophets seemed to occupy a central role in the liturgical assemblies. Whether this refers to the Eucharistic assemblies or simply to agape meals is not clear.

In the fifteenth chapter of the *Didache* mention is made of a more permanent residential ministry that is to assume the functions of the prophets and teachers.

> Appoint for yourselves, then, bishops and deacons who are worthy of the Lord . . . men who are unassuming and not greedy, who are honest and have been proved, for they also are performing for you the task [*leitourgian*] of the prophets and teachers. Therefore, do not despise them, for they are honorable men among you along with the prophets and teachers (15:1-2).[17]

Again, it is difficult to determine the exact content of this "task" (*leitourgia*) of the prophets and teachers, but the assumption is that these ministries are connected with the Word. The question, however, remains: Does this "task" refer to more than preaching or teaching? Mohler describes this *leitourgia* as the office of teaching and presiding.[18] Donovan, while admitting that it was the whole community that offered the Eucharistic sacrifice, sees in this text an indication that certain functions, perhaps the recitation of Eucharistic prayers and the task of presiding, were identified with certain individuals.[19]

The writings of Ignatius of Antioch (d. ca. 117) provide an insight into second-century Syrian Christianity. The basic purpose of his letters was to encourage the different Churches to strive for unity in the face of false doctrines by submitting themselves to the bishop and presbyterate. His letters seem to reflect a clearly defined hierarchical form of ministry consisting of a monarchical bishop, a college of presbyters, and deacons. Furthermore, he places great emphasis on the cultic function of the bishop, for it is in the celebration of the Eucharist that Church unity is principally expressed and realized.[20]

Commentators draw three important observations from the writings of Ignatius. First, there is an evolution in the significance of the titles of office. Whereas in the Pastorals and the first letter of Clement the titles *episkopos* and *presbyteros* are used somewhat interchangeably, here the *episkopos* is clearly the president of the college of elders. Moreover, it is clear that there is a monarchical episcopate in the Churches of Ignatius' correspondence. Finally, not only are specific cultic acts identified by a priestly terminology that before was applied only to Christ and the community, but these acts are centered in specific offices of ministry.

The *Apostolic Tradition* of Hippolytus (d. 235) contains ordination rituals for bishop, presbyter, and deacon. In the prayer for the ordination of a bishop, a distinct parallel between Israel and its institutions and the Church and its ministries is noted. In addition, the emphasis is clearly cultic. The bishop is the high priest, the leader of the community, the liturgical minister who propitiates and offers the gifts of the people to God.

By comparison, while the presbyter is placed among the governing body of the community through ordination, the emphasis in the presbyteral ordination prayer, unlike that for the bishop, is not patently cultic.[21] In spite of the fact that the presbyters occupied places of honor at the liturgy and imposed hands with the bishop over the Eucharistic offerings, it appears that the presbyters seldom exercised this priestly function independently of the bishop, primarily because of the quasi-monopoly the bishop continued to hold on the Eucharistic offering.[22]

The Syrian *Didascalia Apostolorum* depicts the Church order of the East, in which the bishop appears at the center of the community as the high priest and king. Very little mention of presbyters is made in the *Didascalia*, especially in comparison with the treatment of the bishop and deacons. This would seem to indicate the special prominence of these two offices in the East at that time.

With the developing importance of the office of bishop in almost every aspect of Church life, together with the increasing emphasis on the ritual expression of Christian cult as sacrifice, Cyprian of Carthage (d. 258) describes the office of bishop in strong sacerdotal terminology. Although he never explicitly applies the word *sacerdos* to the presbyters, its can be seen from his writings that they were understood as sharing in the sacerdotal office. Cyprian notes that the presbyter, in the absence of the bishop, is to receive the confessions of those dangerously ill and offer the Eucharist.

When the bishop is present, however, the presbyters revert to being a council of elders who give advice.[23]

On the basis of the findings of those who have investigated the order of ministry in the early Church, the conclusion can be drawn that the official threefold hierarchical structure of ministry present in the Church at the time of the Council of Trent was the fruit of a development that became universal throughout the Church sometime during the third century. Moreover, the evidence of the New Testament texts as well as the non-biblical documents examined seems to substantiate the position that the assigning of cultic functions to specific offices and the overall awareness of the functions of the fully evolved offices of ministry as being specifically priestly were likewise the products of development.

Within this process of development, it was also noted, sacramental designations, especially that of presiding at the Eucharist, were first of all extended to bishops and only secondarily, and usually with the specific designation of the bishop, to the presbyters. Thus it appears that it was not until the third century that in the consciousness of the universal Church the office of presbyter carried with it a recognition of certain sacramental responsibilities and powers.

As a result of all of this research, Raymond Brown has made the following observation:

> There is simply no compelling evidence for the classic thesis that the members of the Twelve always presided when they were present, and that there was a chain of ordination passing the power of presiding at the Eucharist from the Twelve to missionary apostles to presbyter-bishop. Although we do not intend to discuss the origin of other priestly powers that were subsequently designated as sacramental, the same lack of evidence would call into question the chain theory of the communication of the power to forgive sins, anoint the sick, etc.[24]

In light of this scholarship, one cannot automatically presume that all the sacramental responsibilities traditionally attributed to one or the other of the hierarchical offices of ministry were determined by the direct institution of Christ or by the Apostles. It seems closer to historical fact to say that it was the Church which in most cases clearly determined what belonged to the various gradations of the public offices of ministry. Consequently, it remains at least an open question whether the early Church understood the "presbyters" mentioned by James to be those officers in the community who were invested with "priestly" powers. This fact further legitimizes any effort to ascertain the precise intention of Trent in defining canon 4 on the minister of extreme unction on the basis of James 5:14.

## Methods of Recent Theological Efforts to Interpret Trent

Traditionally, especially in the "manual theology" prevalent in schools of theology prior to Vatican II, the various canons of Trent that contain an element of presumed Reformation doctrine to which an *anathema sit* had been attached indicated that the teaching in question was to be considered "heretical," as though the contents were a denial of something directly revealed by God. It followed logically that the truth opposed by the error expressed in the canon was to be considered a "dogma of faith," that is, something revealed by God and promulgated by the Church as such, and therefore immutable and irrevocable. If this procedure with regard to the canons of Trent was totally accurate, canon 4 would have to be considered an irreversible obstacle to the Church's appointment of anyone other than the priest to administer the sacrament of anointing.

Recently, however, research into the Council of Trent by a number of scholars has led them to the conclusion that this traditional method of interpreting the Tridentine canons is highly inadequate. Although each of these theologians has approached Trent with specific perspectives and questions in mind, their methodological findings and procedures are indispensable for any accurate interpretation of Tridentine teaching. Moreover, this contemporary scholarship further indicates that canon 4 may not have settled once and for all the question of who can anoint the sick. It is important for the purposes of this study, therefore, to identify some of these more significant hermeneutical insights.

## Sixteenth-century World View

Carl Peter, in treating the Tridentine doctrine on integral auricular confession, makes an observation concerning the world view prevalent at the time of Trent. This view, he claims, had a distinct influence on the way the Council Fathers accepted the practices and institutions of the Church at that time. According to Peter, since the scientific revolution was still in its incipient stages, the mindset prevalent at the time of Trent was that

> nature in and around man was regarded not as the area where he could dominate but rather as something which called for his accommodation. It was understood more in terms of what he was to accept than a perspective of possible modification according to his own designs.[25]

In the face of such a viewpoint, people could choose one or more possible responses: they could conform to or rebel from their condition; they could devise methods whereby they might become more operative within their condition; or they could regard the limitations placed upon them from within and without as "providential indications of the degree of freedom [they were] to exercise and not to exceed in the living of [their] life."[26] Peter notes that often Christian persons of faith adopted the last possibility, looking for God's will in the present state of the institutions around them as well as in the various commands and prohibitions found in the law of the gospel. Historically, it was not until the scientific revolution was fully in force that people came to recognize that many of the limits in their life could be overcome and therefore need not be regarded as divinely established.

This observation is of key importance when it comes to the documents of Trent, especially in order to determine what the Tridentine Fathers considered to be of divine law. At Trent, according to Carl Peter, whatever was expressed "in the Sacred Scriptures and institutions arising from them . . . what followed necessarily from the Scriptures . . . and finally whatever was required for man's salvation at a particular period of history was for that very fact the object of divine law, no matter how much ecclesiastical determination of conditions and details it presupposed."[27] Consequently, for Trent, "divine law" could be used even for ecclesiastical and civil institutions. Peter explains:

> An obligation can come from God because at a particular period of history its object is necessary for man if he is to enjoy the conditions as required for salvation. In that period, God really expects of those concerned the fulfillment of what is necessary, and the latter is of divine law.[28]

As a result of Peter's findings, sensitivity must be paid to the possibility that the contents of at least some of the canons, though taught by Trent as expressive of the "divine will" and therefore "dogmas of faith," may not be so in the way in which these concepts have been defined by the later official teaching of the Church and are understood today.

## The Tridentine Documents and the Reformation

A more obvious conclusion that can be drawn from the historical context of Trent is that one of the essential purposes of the Council was to respond to the errors and heresies of the Reformers. Thus the documents of Trent were, in the words of R. Aubert, "fortuitously engendered."[29] By this he means that the pronouncements of Trent were culturally determined both in language and in the level of theological research and thought patterns out of which they arose. Furthermore, considering that these pronouncements were occasioned by a particular historical situation to which the Church had to respond in order to reaffirm a truth under attack or in danger of neglect, these documents often represent a partial and particular teaching on a certain question. It cannot be said that in each and every case it was the intention of Trent to say all that could be said on a particular subject, and there can be instances where the teaching of Trent requires completion.

Moreover, Hubert Jedin, Piet Fransen, and Carl Peter are all of the opinion that the most profound point that divided the Reformers from the Catholics was their respective concepts of the Church, not only concerning its hierarchical structure but above all its intimate nature as the bearer of truth and grace and its claim to be the supreme authority in all things that pertain to salvation.³⁰ Fransen observes that at the time of Trent

> the Lutherans, when they recognzied it [the power of the Church], claimed that it could only be exercised in the pure and simple application of the Gospel. The Church in any case could never oblige the consciences of men . . . the Church, on the contrary, claimed to have received all the power from Christ to oblige in conscience Christians to accept from Christ all truth necessary for salvation. These truths have been contained in the Gospel and also in the tradition of the Church, divine tradition, apostolic or ecclesiastical.³¹

Given this fact, Fransen concludes that Trent, in directing itself against what it understood to be the errors and heresies of the Lutherans, "defined the limits within which the outlook of our faith remains orthodox by simply excluding views which have no place."³² Nevertheless, it remains an open question whether, in the case of a particular definition, these limits have been traced to the fullest extent, so that no additional development or reform is possible.

### Trent: "Heresy," "Anathema sit," and "Faith"

Contemporary scholarship also notes that Trent seemed to have a multivalent understanding and use of the concepts "heresy," "anathema," and "faith." It is principally this factor that illustrates the inadequacy of most of the uncritical use of the Tridentine documents.

The contemporary theological understanding of the terms noted above stems from Chapter 3 of Vatican I, where the Council speaks of the object of faith.

> Further, by divine and Catholic faith, all those things must be believed which are contained in the written word of God and in tradition, and which are proposed by the Church either in solemn pronouncement or in her ordinary and universal teaching power to be believed as divinely revealed (DS 3011).

In short, as Fransen writes, "Faith today is that which is directly revealed by God (explicitly or implicitly) and promulgated as such by the Magisterium of the Church (ordinary or extraordinary)."³³ It appears that Vatican I left undefined the precise status of those truths which, though not revealed, are so intimately connected with revelation that if they were denied, one's faith would be endangered. It is the contention of many authors today that in Trent the notions of "faith" and "heresy," though including the contemporary understanding as defined by Vatican I, could have had a wider meaning in certain cases.

This position is substantiated by the writings of the sixteenth-century theologian Melchior Cano, who himself attended Trent. In his classic work *De locis theologicis*, Cano offers an insight into the mentality of at least a number of the theologians at that time concerning these concepts. In Book XII he discusses theological conclusions and states that there are two classes of propositions of faith: those that pertain to faith immediately and those that pertain mediately. The first category are "those that are the legitimate principles of theology, of which they may be either primary or secondary, that is, those that God himself revealed to the Church, or the second class being those that are collected necessarily from the first."[34]

Regarding propositions pertaining mediately to the faith, there are also two classes:

> One class is of conclusions which arise solely from principles of faith. The other is those which faith alone does not confect without the aid of external disciplines, but which are acquired either from one or many principles known by natural reason. But these, even if not on the same plane and grade, can simply and without addition all be called questions of faith.[35]

After describing what can properly be considered theological conclusions, Cano makes the following significant observation:

> If either the Church or a council of the Apostolic See or even the saints universally with one mind and voice confect some theological conclusion and prescribe it for the faithful, this conclusion will be so considered to be *"veritas Catholica"* as if it had been revealed by Christ, and those who deny it will be considered equal to a heretic as if they were opposing the sacred writings and Apostolic traditions. I refer here properly to a conclusion of theology that is deduced by a certain and firm connection from the principles of this faculty.[36]

Thus it is seen that in the sixteenth century it was common to use the terms "faith" and "heresy" in a more inclusive sense, which incorporated, according to Cano, even those theological conclusions that arise out of principles of faith.

Furthermore, since the primary purpose of the Council was to defend the authority and practice of the Church against the attacks of the Reformers, a number of canons are found whose contents are clearly not of the original deposit of revelation but to which an *"anathema sit"* was attached. Some examples would include DS 1657, regarding the practice of reserving the Eucharist; DS 1732, on the administration of Holy Communion under both kinds; DS 1757, on the use of vestments and outward signs.

What must always be kept in mind in any effort to accurately interpret the documents of Trent is the fact that the Council understood that its task was, first and foremost, to defend the Church against the Reformers' obstinate spirit, out of which arose their accusations that the Church had erred in its teaching and practice. As Cano observed, *"pertinacia* (obstinacy) is at the heart of heresy . . . heresy is a vice not only of the intellect, but also of the will."[37] For Trent, the *contumacia* (insolent stubbornness) of the Reformers arose from their formal disobedience of rebellion and their obstinate refusal to submit to the Church's authority in matters pertaining to salvation. According to Fransen,

> the heretic was the rebel par excellence; excommunication, and in particular anathema, was the *"mucro episcopalis"* (episcopal weapon) par excellence against all those who refused to submit to the authority instituted by Christ, episcopal and papal.[38]

Consequently, the Fathers at Trent used the anathema to strike out at this contumacious attitude of the Reformers.

As a result of all of these findings, it is clear that Trent frequently anathematized various positions of the Reformers as being "heretical" even though the contents of these teachings may not have been heresy in the modern sense of a formal and immediate denial of a point of revealed doctrine. The heresy of the Reformers in these cases was the fact that they maliciously attacked and denied the power and authority of the Church, and accused the Church of having erred in a particular matter.

By the same token, Trent's understanding of "faith" included not only what was revealed by God and promulgated as such by the Church as we understand the term "faith" today, but it also could incorporate all that the Church has declared as binding upon the Christian as necessary for salvation. Among such things would be not only "theological truths" deduced from the primary principles of faith but even universally applicable ecclesiastical laws, which were likewise considered to be "necessary for salvation." Therefore, any study of Tridentine teaching must include a careful investigation of whatever canons are in question to see if their doctrinal content is a dogma of faith as we understand "faith" today, or if Trent defined it in the wider sense of the terms "faith" and "heresy," which then could admit the possibility of change or development.

With particular reference to canon 4, the problem is clearly defined: Does this canon represent a "dogma of faith" according to the understanding of Vatican I, a denial of which would be heretical in the strict sense of the term? Or was canon 4 a reaffirmation of an accepted practice of the Church, a defiance of which would be insolent and disruptive, and therefore "heretical" in a broader sense? If the latter is the case, then it would be entirely possible that canon 4 no longer need be accepted as a necessary obstacle to the Church's appointment of someone other than the priest as a minister of the sacramental anointing of the sick.

*Chapter Two*

## THE ANOINTING OF THE SICK
## IN THE FIRST FOUR CENTURIES

In order to interpret accurately the Tridentine teaching on extreme unction, especially canon 4 on the proper minister of the sacrament, it is of great importance that the deliberations of the Council be seen in light of both their remote and more immediate historical context. The remote context, the history of the preceding fifteen centuries, demonstrates the development of the Church's understanding and practice regarding the sacramental anointing of the sick.

### The Ministry to the Sick in the New Testament

*Background for understanding the ministry to the sick in the New Testament*

A common Old Testament attitude traces a cause-effect relationship between sin and the demonic powers and the related effects of illness and other maladies (see, for example, the canticle of Hezekiah in Isaiah 38:9-20). Within this framework Yahweh is considered the source of healing, and prayer to Yahweh becomes a principal means whereby one achieves relief from afflictions (e.g., Pss 6; 16:10; 30:2; 32:3; 41:4; 51:7). As the Old Testament revelation progressed, the notion of sickness as a divinely ordered test as well as an opportunity for the perfection of virtue and a means of discipline came more to the fore (Isa 53).

Although the relation between sin and sickness persisted even into New Testament times (Matt 12:22; Luke 11:14; 13:11; John 5:14; 9:1ff., et al.), one of Jesus' contributions was to interject into this rather rigid Jewish notion of retribution the expiatory function of illness (Matt 16:24-25; Mark 8:34-35) and to demonstrate that suffering of this sort can also be accepted as redounding to the glory of God (John 9; 11:3-4). These new dimensions, however, never obscured the New Testament consciousness of sickness as being a sign of the fundamental disorder introduced into the human condition by sin. Consequently, the cures effected by Jesus, in addition to authenticating his mission as the envoy of God, were signs of his task of liberating humanity from the power of evil and thereby overthrowing the kingdom of Satan and manifesting the presence of the kingdom of God.

Jesus bestowed upon his disciples a share in his healing power and commissioned them to go among the people as witnesses and heralds of the same kingdom he himself was announcing. Essential in the apostolic ministry of healing was the place of prayer (Mark 9:27-28) and calling on the name of Jesus (Luke 10:17-19). It was only in faith and on the authority and the power of Jesus that the disciples found success in combating the powers of darkness and were able to call attention, especially by their cures and other miracles, to the presence of God's kingdom.

A common practice in both the Hellenistic and the Jewish world of that time was the anointing of the sick with oil. The pagans looked upon the use of oil not only as having medicinal value but also as part of magical and religious practices. The uses of anointing the sick in the New Testament period were varied. At times it was purely medicinal (Luke 10:34); at other times it was employed for a combination of medicinal and exorcistic purposes, and oftentimes it accompanied the purely charismatic acts of healing performed by the Apostles. Only one reference is found in the New Testament (James 5:14-15) in which an anointing of the sick with oil appears to be more institutional in nature rather than a type of "home remedy" or charismatic healing.

*Mark 6:13*

> So they [the Twelve] set off to preach repentance; and they cast out many devils, and anointed many sick people with oil and cured them.[1]

Although in parallel references (Matt 10:1; Luke 9:1) the other synoptic writers mention these apostolic cures carried out on the direct mandate of Jesus as part of the Apostles' general mission to preach penance, forgiveness, and the kingdom, only Mark specifies that in curing the sick the Apostles anointed them with oil.

The Semitic consciousness of the relation between sickness and the demonic powers, as well as the linking of the exorcising of the possessed with the curing of the sick, emphasizes the spiritual nature of the kingdom preached by the Apostles, of which these acts were signs. At the same time, it should be kept in mind that the Hebrew mentality was especially sensitive to the concept of the human person as a unity of body and soul. The philosophical and mystical separation of the human person into the essential elements of body and soul was largely foreign to the Jews throughout the biblical period. Thus the importance of the physical effect achieved by the miraculous cures of the Apostles must not be overlooked. A more balanced view would lead to the conclusion that the ministry of the Apostles cannot be seen as totally physical or totally spiritual.

There has been considerable debate down through the centuries over the exact relationship between this Marcan text and the origin of the Church's sacramental anointing of the sick. From the highly charismatic nature of these cures wherein the effectiveness of the use of oil is centered to a great degree around the individual applying the oil, the Apostles appear to act more as thaumaturges, or wonder-workers. Thus it would seem that their anointing of the sick as attested to in Mark 6:13 can only be accepted, at most, as a figure or type of the sacramental rite that is ecclesial and more institutional in nature.

*James 5:14-15*

> If one of you is ill, he should send for the presbyters of the Church and they are to anoint him with oil in the name of the Lord and

pray over him. The prayer of faith will save the sick man and the Lord will raise him up again; and if he has committed any sins, he will be forgiven.[2]

From the text itself, it is seen that James addresses himself to sickness in general. While in the New Testament the term *asthenes* is used to indicate some sort of physical malady (e.g., Matt 10:8; 25:36; Mark 6:56; Luke 4:40; John 4:46), the degree of seriousness of this illness is not indicated. The fact that the infirm person is unable to leave his bed might indicate that although he is not necessarily at the point of death, he is not suffering from just any slight illness. The consciousness of the prospective recipient seems to be implied, for the text states that it is the sick person who sends for the presbyters of the Church.

The key question for the purposes of this study is: Who are the "presbyters of the Church" who are to be sent for? It has already been noted that according to recent scholarship, the New Testament usage of the term "presbyter," while not simply denoting one who is an "elder" in terms of age, does refer to a title of dignity similar to that held by the college of elders in the Jewish synagogue. Thus it would appear that the presbyters are those persons in the Christian community recognized as having some specific office or function of leadership.[3]

The use of the definite article "the" with "presbyters" could be intended to set apart those particular individuals who by virtue of their position were recognized as having the power or the responsibility of performing this ritual prescribed by James. The descriptive phrase "of the Church" might also identify these elders as belonging to the same particular Christian community as the sick person. The plural "presbyters" can be explained either by the more obvious meaning of the word that "many presbyters" are to be summoned, or it could be an indication, in a general fashion, of the certain group of individuals described above, one of whom is to come and to anoint. Regardless of how these words are to be understood, nothing in the text indicates that the presbyters to be called are those looked upon as possessing a charismatic gift of healing.

The ritual to be performed is described by James as consisting of an anointing with oil and prayer over the sick person. The use of the aorist tense in the instruction "to pray over the sick person" implies that the prayer either precedes the act of anointing or takes place during it. The exact meaning of praying "over" the person is also somewhat vague. It could refer either to the need to pray for the intentions of the patient, or perhaps it could have a local sense indicating that the presbyters gathered around the sick person stretch out or even impose their hands on him. Exactly what words were used in this prayer cannot be deduced from the text of James. It appears to be deprecatory, uttered in favor of the subject of the ritual. The phrase "in the name of the Lord" might indicate that the name of Jesus is invoked in the prayer, or it may simply be a reference to the fact that the anointing is done on the order of Jesus with faith in his name. There are commentators who admit the possibility that this phrase, instead of referring to the prayer or ritual action, may be a qualification of the oil used in the anointing, thereby inferring that the oil is itself blessed in the name of the Lord.

Verse 15 lists the effects of this ritual: "The prayer of faith will save the sick man." Again the phrase "prayer of faith" is general and admits of one or more possible meanings. It could indicate that the prayer of the presbyters requires, and is accompanied by, faith. It could be an allusion to the fact that the ritual receives its efficacy from the faith of the whole community, represented by the presbyters, or from the faith of the sick person being anointed. There is also the question of whether James attributes the effects mentioned to the prayer, to the anointing, or to both combined.

What is meant by "will save the sick man"? The Greek word *sozein* is used by James in other places in his letter (1:21; 2:14; 4:12; 5:20) to denote a salvation that points to or consists of eternal life. Other New Testament uses of this same verb (e.g., Matt 9:21; Mark 5:28; 6:56; 10:52; Luke 8:48) include, unlike the other references from James, a physical dimension, as is seen especially from their context, which is concerned with sickness. The question remains, Does the traditional text from James refer to the health of both the body and the soul? Since James 5:14-15 is concerned with the concrete case of a person who is ill, and recalling the Jewish mindset of viewing the whole person as well as seeing the relationship between sickness and sin, it would seem that the best interpretation of *sozein* here is the restoration or salvation of the whole person, body and soul.

In what sense, then, will the Lord "raise him up?" In 1 Corinthians 15:15, 29, 32, 35, 42-44; 2 Corinthians 1:9; 4:14, *egerein* has the meaning of "raising from the dead." In other texts where this same verb is used (e.g., Matt 9:5-7, 25; Mark 1:31; 2:9; 5:41; 9:27), the significance is a "raising to life and health." There is considerable disagreement among commentators on the nature of this "raising up" as it is used in James. For many it pertains to a spiritual strengthening whereby there is an increase of faith and a liberation from the fear and anxiety that often attack a person at the time of illness. As with *sozein*, perhaps a combination of both interpretations is again more accurate.

The final part of verse 15 mentions another possible effect: "If he has committed any sins, he will be forgiven." James seems to refer to this effect as conditional. If so, one may infer that James does not always see a causal connection between sin and sickness. It cannot be concluded from the text whether James is referring to venial or more serious sins. In reality, to look for such a specification would be somewhat anachronistic, for it is a distinction that would have been unknown to him.

## The Anointing of the Sick in the Non-biblical Writings of the First Four Centuries

### *Charismatic anointings*

While there are no Scripture commentaries from this period on either the traditional Marcan or James texts, Hilary of Poitiers commented on Matt 10:1-8, which is considered to be a parallel to Mark 6:13. In his commentary,[4] Hilary observes the conferral of power by Jesus upon his Apostles and the various miracles executed by them, including the curing of the sick. All these miracles were associated with the apostolic mission to preach the kingdom of God. Clearly charismatic in nature, these miracles, including the cures, are principally of sign value. John Chrysostom, in two homilies on the same verse from Matthew,[5] emphasizes this sign value of the cures and reiterates that they flowed not from power proper to the Apostles as men but from a gift freely bestowed upon them by the Lord.

There are also a number of hagiographic accounts that refer to the Desert Fathers, who performed miraculous cures with the use of oil.[6] Frequently the maladies cured by these holy men were associated with diabolic possession, and often oil was used simply in order to exorcise a demonic spirit. The maladies mentioned vary in nature from different forms of sickness, to paralysis, to loss of one or more of the senses, and to deformity.[7]

While all these documents mention the common elements of the ritual prescribed by James (prayer and an anointing with oil), nowhere is the use of this oil referred specifically to the text of James. Clearly the effects resulting from the anointing are described as being miraculous in nature and refer to the charismatic gift of healing.

## Response to the erroneous practices of the heretics

There are several writers dating from these early centuries who addressed various erroneous practices of different heretical factions. In Book 1 of his *Contra haereses*, Irenaeus speaks out against the practice of the Marcionites, who anointed their dead with oil and water.[8] This particular attack was part of Irenaeus' general polemic against the Gnostics, who in their cultic functions frequently juxtaposed superstitious practices derived from the pagans with various Christian rites. Irenaeus does not explain exactly what this Marcionite rite was, nor can it be definitively concluded that this reference is indirect proof of the presence in the Christian Church of a rite of anointing the dying that was being imitated by the heretics.

Tertullian, in his *Liber de praescriptionibus*, notes a number of practices of the heretics that were considered to be abuses. He specifically speaks out against their granting of sacerdotal functions to the laity, and especially permitting their women to teach, perform exorcisms, and promise cures.[9] The "promise of cures" referred to here was probably considered to be institutional or hierarchical in nature, for certainly he would have been aware that charisms of healing could be granted to the laity as well as to priests. It cannot be determined, however, what the exact action of the curing was. At most, his reference to this particular heretical abuse might only be an allusion to a ritual act of curing practiced by the Church at that time.

In his *De poenitentia*, Ambrose attempts to demonstrate the inconsistency of the Novatians, who denied that the priest had the power to forgive sins, even though their own ministers baptized and imposed hands on the sick.[10] He notes from Mark 16:17 that the Lord had given power to the disciples so that when they cast out devils, released the dumb, and "imposed hands on the sick," their human operations were rendered efficacious by God. Again, it is unclear whether Ambrose is referring to this imposition of hands as a charismatic act of healing or to a sacramental administration to the sick. Although it is possible to see how an imposition of hands is inferred from James 5:14, there is no evidence that this was the way the ritual prescribed by James was referred to at this time.

*The Church's ministry to the sick and dying*

In 1963 a Bedouin discovered a silver lamina upon which is inscribed in Aramaic a description of the anointing of an infirm person.[11] It has been estimated that the lamina comes from the end of the first century and is therefore contemporary with the Epistle of James. According to a recent interpretation, the lamina refers to the "oil of faith," which title is similar to the Eastern name for the ritual anointing of the sick. The account contains a deprecatory invocation, "in the Name," and the anointing is performed by an act of sprinkling with a sprig of hyssop. There is a series of rubrical signs, one of which appears to signify the use of the sign of the cross, probably in the act of sprinkling. The effect expected is the relief of the fallen person from the suffering that has come upon him/her as the debt of sin.

It would be hasty to conclude that this is an example of the rite prescribed by James. The newly discovered lamina is, however, evidence of a very early religious anointing with oil for the purpose of obtaining a cure. Whether the intended healing was simply physical or both physical and spiritual is difficult to ascertain, for the spiritual references may only be examples of the Jewish practice of attributing physical maladies to sin.

Among the *Canons of Hippolytus*, which date from the end of the third century, six deal with the ministry to the sick.[12] In particular, canons 199 and 200 describe the visit of a bishop to a sick person. While the ceremonial for this visitation is not given, the canon does instruct that the bishop "pray over the sick person," which may be a possible allusion to James. The bishop's prayer seems to have a curative character, since it is explicitly linked to an episode from the Scriptures where the shadow of Peter cured the sick.

In canon 219 the sick are instructed to frequent the church so that "they may enjoy the prayer." An exception is made for those who are dangerously ill; they may remain at home and be visited by a cleric. The canon does not state, however, exactly what the "prayer" was that took place in the church.

Even though there is no explicit mention of an anointing of the sick made in the canons, a possible indirect reference may be found in canon 222, which is concerned with the preparation of the vases "necessary for the sick," thereby alluding to the vases that may have contained the oil used in such anointings.

Canon 13 of the First Council of Nicaea (325) clearly speaks of the obligation of administering Viaticum to the dying—even to excommunicated persons who are on their deathbed.[13] This decree demonstrates, first of all, the evident importance the Church placed on the administration of Viaticum. Secondly, no mention is made of any anointing in the ministry to the dying, which would seem to imply that in the minds of the Nicaean Fathers, only Viaticum was considered to be the sacrament of the dying.

*Penitential anointings*

There are two controversial documents dating from this early period that contain a clear but enigmatic reference to James 5:14-15. In his second homily on Leviticus,[14] Origen lists seven ways of obtaining pardon in the New Law, the last of which is penance. In his description of penance, he indicates the need for the sinner to have remorse, to confess his/her sins to the priest, and then to ask for a remedy so that what was written by James (5:14-15) might be fulfilled.

The question arises: Is Origen referring to the sacrament of penance or to that of anointing? He makes a significant textual change when, in citing James, he replaces "let them pray over him" with the words "they impose hands on him." The exact reason for this change is unclear. Is Origen attributing the remission of sins to a penitential rite that in his time may have included an imposition of hands, or is it the result of an anointing specifically directed to the sick?

There is one school of opinion[15] which holds that Origen's text refers to the sacrament of penance and that he is interpreting James allegorically to imply that the infirmity is the "sickness of sin," which is to be healed by the priest. The problem with this interpretation centers around the meaning of the anointing mentioned by James and quoted by Origen. While an anointing of penitents for the remission of sins was practiced in certain areas of the East, there is no evidence that this was the custom at the time of Origen.

A second opinion[16] holds that Origen had in mind either an infirm penitent or a sinner who falls seriously ill before completing laborious penance, so that the reference here is to extreme unction, which, as the consummation of penance, is one of the ways in the New Law for remitting sins. This interpretation, however, fails to explain not only Origen's reason for tampering with the text of James but also the fact that he makes no mention of any physical effect derived from this ritual.

A second document is likewise an inconclusive reference to the sacrament of extreme unction. John Chrysostom (ca. 347–407) praises the excellence of the priesthood in his *De sacerdotio*, and he delineates the various powers conferred upon priests.[17] Among these powers, he notes the power of the priest to forgive sins, and he refers it to James 5:14-15. The same question surfaces here as in the case of Origen: In citing James, is Chrysostom referring the text to the sacrament of penance or to extreme unction? There are the same two schools of interpretation, and again neither opinion is fully satisfactory.

A clear reference to a penitential anointing is found in the Council of Laodicea (367), which describes the process by which those converted from heresy were readmitted into the Church. After renouncing all heresy, especially that to which they had once ascribed, the penitents were to recite the Creed, be anointed with oil, and then communicate.[18] It should be noted, however, that nowhere does the Council, unlike Origen and Chrysostom, refer this practice of anointing in the reconciliation of heretics specifically to James 5.

*Liturgical documentation*

Probably the most important non-biblical documents of these early centuries are several liturgical texts for the blessing of oil. Unfortunately these texts are not always clear regarding the significance of the oil or of the anointing mentioned.

The *Apostolic Tradition* of Hippolytus (ca. 170–235) contains the most ancient reference to the oil of the sick. The text was originally written in Greek and was translated into Coptic, Arabic, and Ethiopian; the Latin translation dates from the fifth century. The blessing of the oil appears as an appendix to the Eucharistic Prayer and is pronounced by the bishop.[19] God is asked to endow the oil with a power of healing that is exercised when the oil is used either internally, apparently as a drink, or externally by anointing. Furthermore, the location of this blessing within the anaphora of the Mass is important. Later tradition blessed the oil of the sick on Holy Thursday in the same place during the liturgy, a fact which in itself could be indirect evidence that the oil blessed by this formula in the *Apostolic Tradition* was considered to be this same oil of the sick.

The Ethiopian translation of the Greek formula contains two important variances from the Latin. Whereas the Latin reads, "As you sanctify this oil may you grant to all who *use* and receive it . . .," the Ethiopian text has, "to all who are anointed and receive of it."[20] Although the Ethiopian "to all who are anointed" indicates a mode of "using" the oil, the Latin translation seems to imply the possibility in a more active sense of the people "using" or administering the oil themselves.

The second variance concerns the effects expected from the use of the oil. The Latin has "may it give *health* to all that use it," while the Ethiopian renders "to offer health" as "sanctify." Again, the Latin translation appears to recognize, if not even emphasize, the physical effect resulting from the use of the oil, while the other reading underscores the spiritual nature of the effect.

The reference to the internal use of the oil has been interpreted in different ways. Some authors are of the opinion that at least some of the blessed oil was returned to the faithful for their own use.[21] The drinking of the oil by the laity would then be considered a devotional practice. Therefore, according to these authors, the one formula was for the blessing of oil destined for a twofold usage—one sacramental by the priests, the other private by the faithful.

A second interpretation holds that this oil, blessed by the bishop and thereby rendered capable of producing the indicated effects, was used equally and for the same purpose by the priests and the laity.[22] Consequently, the oil is not directed toward a twofold usage, and there is no need to appeal to a distinction between one use that is devotional and private, and another that is a sacrament.

In the *Sacramentary of Serapion,* two prayers to be recited over oil are found.[23] The first prayer is one of a group of five said during the Eucharistic celebration. According to the text of the first prayer, God is asked to bestow curative power upon the "water and oil so that every fever, demon and disease may be removed through drink and anointing." In such a way it is prayed that the reception of this oil may be a "remedy of cure and of integrity." It appears from this prayer that both water and oil are placed on the same level, for the blessing is directed to both elements and the effects are expected from the use of both.

The second prayer is located among prayers for baptism, for the imposition of hands over deacons, priests, and bishops, and prayers for the dead, which seems to indicate that it is a blessing of oil for liturgical usage. While the title of the prayer is listed as

"Prayer for oil of the sick or for bread or for water," only the blessing of the oil is mentioned in the text of the prayer. The formula contains a long list of effects attributed to the use of this blessed oil, effects that are of both the physical and the spiritual order. Even though it makes no specific mention of the text of James, almost all Catholic commentators are in agreement that this second formula refers to the blessing of oil used in the conferral of extreme unction.

A significant question arises from these blessings: What is the nature of the use of the oil blessed by the first formula? According to some authors, this oil is not that of extreme unction, both because of the union of the oil with water and because it is returned to the faithful to be taken home and used there. Thus the oil mentioned here is solely for private use.[24]

Others are either of the opinion that each of the two formulas was used for the blessing of oil destined for both sacramental and devotional purposes,[25] or they see no essential difference between the oil blessed by either of these prayers.[26] According to this latter position, it is the "oil of prayer" that the sick person receives from the Church. In neither blessing is there a specific reference that an anointing with this oil is necessarily to be done by priests. Both formulas refer to the temporal and spiritual effects expected from the use of this oil, and there does not appear to be any reason for not accepting that the oil blessed by either formula was for sacramental purposes.

In the document *Testamentum Domini nostri Jesu Christi,* there is found a prayer for the blessing of oil to be used for "the cure of those who suffer."[27] This same prayer is also said over water. The formula specifies those for whom it is being prepared and the effects intended: ". . . send upon this oil, which is a type of your abundance, the complement of your beneficent mercy that it might free those laboring, heal the sick and sanctify those returning when they enter upon your faith." It is not evident from the text whether this blessed oil is destined not only for an anointing of the sick but also for the anointing of catechumens. The blessing also leaves unanswered the question: Is the efficacy attributed to the oil also expected from the water so blessed?

## Observations Regarding Anointing in the First Four Centuries

It is interesting to observe that while the New Testament contains a concise description of a ritual anointing of the sick, the non-biblical documents of this early period contain very few references to this rite as it is prescribed in the Epistle of James. Furthermore, while a number of texts indicate a Christian ministry to the sick in which an anointing with oil was included, it is not always clear as to whether or not this was understood to be a sacramental anointing. In addition to penitential anointings, there were instances where this anointing was charismatic in nature, used to cure people from a variety of infirmities, including demonic possession. Nowhere, however, was it found that an anointing with oil was restricted only to the dying. In fact, as canon 13 of the Council of Nicaea demonstrates, the Church considered Viaticum as the necessary sacrament for the dying.

With the exception of the controverted texts of Ambrose, Origen, and Chrysostom, whenever the anointing is clearly that administered to the sick, the effects attributed to it appear to be principally physical, with frequent allusions to spiritual effects. Only one of the prayers in the *Sacramentary of Serapion* contains an explicit mention of the remission of sins, and then as part of a long list of effects, the majority of which are of the physical order.

It is especially important to note that the liturgical documents indicate that persons other than priests used the same blessed oil for anointing in cases of sickness. Moreover, these texts make no distinction between the effects intended when the oil was used by priests and those expected when used by the laity.

A number of authors have tried to explain the non-sacerdotal anointings by applying the distinction between a sacrament, which would be the anointing administered by priests, and a sacramental, which would be that done by the laity. It should be noted, however, that sacramental theology was not highly developed in these early centuries. Caution is advised, therefore, when attributing a distinction that is later in origin to the understanding of practices of the Church during the first four centuries.

Finally, although the liturgical blessing by the bishop of the oil used for anointing the sick was considerably organized during this period, no liturgical rituals can be found for the application of this oil. This observation admits of several possible interpretations. It could be that the efficacy of such an anointing was attributed more to the act of consecration of the oil than to its administration. If this is true, it might explain the apparent lack of concern during this early period over who is the proper person to administer the anointing. In addition, if this blessed oil was sacramentally used by the laity as well as by priests, it does not seem that there would be a need for an organized liturgical ritual for anointing.

*Chapter Three*

# THE ANOINTING OF THE SICK FROM INNOCENT I TO THE CAROLINGIAN REFORM

In the preceding chapter it was noted that while the New Testament contains a precise prescription for an institutional anointing with oil to be performed by the Church on behalf of anyone who is ill, the non-biblical documents of the first four centuries contain only vague references to any anointing of the sick. In comparison to the apostolic instruction, the texts are very imprecise as to both the nature and the purpose of this anointing, and only a few of them specifically refer this practice to that found in James 5:14-15.

Beginning with the fifth century, however, numerous documents appear that clearly speak of an ecclesiastical anointing of the sick which is not charismatic in nature and which finds its origins in the words of James. Although these texts are frequently confusing with regard to different aspects of this anointing, they are testimony to the fact that there was a development in the Church's understanding and practice with regard to this particular ritual.

## Letter of Pope Innocent I to Decentius, March 19, 416

The letter of Pope Innocent I to Decentius, bishop of Gubbio, is undoubtedly one of the most important documents in the development of the Church's anointing of the sick as prescribed by James. In addition to the fact that the letter is an authentic document of the Holy See, it is an excellent example of a local bishop consulting the Bishop of Rome, who, on the basis of an interpretation of a particular passage of Scripture, issued a doctrinal/disciplinary statement about a sacramental practice in the Church.

Furthermore, Pope Innocent's reply was quoted by a number of later writers and was included in several canonical collections of the Roman Church prior to the ninth century as an authority substantiating a particular understanding concerning this practice of the Church. It can be safely concluded, therefore, that the papal letter was known throughout the Church in the West during the centuries prior to the Carolingian Reform.

It appears from the context of the letter that Innocent was responding to a question posed by Decentius on the proper interpretation of James 5:14-15, especially with regard to the recipient and minister of the anointing described therein.[1] Innocent writes:

> Since your love prompts you to seek advice on this as on other matters, my son Celestine the deacon also mentioned in his letter that Your Excellency had put up for discussion the text in the epistle of St. James the Apostle: "If anyone among you is sick, let him call the presbyters, and let them pray over him, anointing him with oil in the name of the Lord. And the prayer of faith will save the sick man, and the Lord will restore him, and if he has sinned, He will forgive him" (James 5:14-15). There is no doubt that this ought to be understood of the faithful who are sick and who can be anointed with the holy oil of chrism which, confected by a bishop, is permitted not only to priests but also to all Christians to use for anointing in their own need or that of those close to them. [. . . permitted not only to priests but also to all Christians who *may be anointed* in their own necessity or that of those close to them.] However, it seems to Us that an idle point is raised when doubt is expressed in the case of a bishop about something that is said of priests. For the very reason that it was said of priests is that bishops are burdened with other business and are not able to go to all the sick. However, if a bishop is able or thinks someone worthy of a visit from him, then he, whose duty it is to prepare the chrism, can without any hesitation bless and anoint the sick with chrism. But the chrism cannot be poured on those doing penance because it is of the genus of a sacrament. How is it conceivable that one sacrament can be granted to a person to whom the rest of the sacraments are denied? (DS 216)[2]

It is clear from the particular questions posed to the Pope that Innocent's intention was not to treat exhaustively all the aspects of this ritual practice. This would explain, beyond the Scripture text itself, why he says nothing about the effects of the anointing. It can also be argued that the spiritual nature of the ritual is strongly implied by his insistence on the necessity of the oil being consecrated by a bishop and by his conclusion that the oil is of the "genus of a sacrament."[3]

Innocent refers to the consecrated oil used in this ministry to the sick as the "oil of chrism." The apparent confusion here is explained by the fact that at this time, as evidenced by other documents of this period, the term "chrism" had the more generic sense of "blessed oil" rather than the technical meaning that it has today as a mixture of oil and balsam used in the celebration of baptism, confirmation, and orders.[4]

In response to the first question regarding who may receive this anointing, Innocent interprets the Apostle's words as meaning the faithful who are sick. Although the text indicates that the ritual took place in the home of the recipient, the papal letter says nothing about the specific degree of severity necessary for a person to be anointed, and certainly there is no indication that the anointing is only for the faithful who are in danger of death.[5]

The Pope distinguishes the "faithful who are sick" from those penitents who have been excommunicated and are denied the reception of the sacraments. Also implied is a distinction between these "faithful who are sick" and the catechumens who are likewise not permitted to receive the sacraments.

Concerning Decentius' second question, as to whether the bishop can administer this anointing, Innocent follows two lines of reasoning, each of which clearly indicates his positive response. He argues that if it is the function of the bishop to consecrate the oil to be used in each instance of anointing, *a fortiori* he has the right to administer it, even if, because of his numerous obligations, he is unable to visit the sick himself, thereby necessitating that this ritual ordinarily be performed by the presbyters.

It is in his second argument that a formidable difficulty has arisen over the proper translation and understanding of the Latin words *non solum sacerdotibus, sed et omnibus uti christianis licet in sua aut in suorum necessitate ungendum* in the letter. Two questions present themselves from the text as it stands. Is the Pope saying that in addition to priests who anoint, all Christians also can *administer* this oil confected by a bishop by anointing themselves or members of their families when necessary? If that is what Innocent is saying—and several liturgical documents of the previous centuries make such an interpretation plausible—is this anointing considered to be the same as that of which James wrote and which is administered by the priests? Innocent's letter does not give a clear answer to these questions, and different schools of opinion have tried to clarify this apparent difficulty.

The first such school (e.g., Tapper, Netzer, Kern) interprets the words of Innocent in a passive sense as saying, ". . . is permitted not only to priests but also to all the Christian faithful *who may be anointed* in their own need or that of those close to them."[6] The obvious problem with this position is that it is not grammatically faithful to the text of the letter, which was written as if it should be read in an active sense.

A second opinion (e.g., De Sainte-Beuve, Bord, Ruch, De Letter, Poschmann)[7] understands the words in the active sense as reading: ". . . is permitted not only to priests but also to all Christians to use for anointing in their own need or that of those close to them." This opinion, however, sees these words as referring to a twofold usage of oil: sacramental when administered by a member of the sacerdotal hierarchy, or private and devotional when used by the laity. According to these theologians, the context of the letter demonstrates that Innocent is addressing himself to an anointing that is sacerdotally administered. In other words, the Pope is saying that since priests administer it, so too can bishops, even though they are not always free to visit the sick. This school recognizes that this same oil is also available to the laity for their private use in an effort to seek cures of their maladies, similar to the way in which the faithful use holy water and other blessed objects. This lay anointing would not be that prescribed by James or of the same order as that administered by priests and bishops.

Although this opinion remains grammatically faithful to the words of Innocent and acknowledges a lay anointing that was implied in the liturgical documents of the previous centuries, the problem still remains: In light of the text of the letter, what is the basis upon which the distinction is made between a sacramental anointing and a devotional one? Innocent speaks here only of one anointing. Even though it is applied by different persons, it nevertheless involves the usage of the same blessed oil. It is referred to the same text of Scripture, and there is attributed to it the effects delineated by James. It would appear that the only way in which such a distinction could legitimately be applied would be if there were evidence that the difference between a sacrament and a sacramental was so well known by the Church at Rome in the fifth century that Innocent could have presupposed that his reference to lay anointing would have been so understood.

The third school (e.g., Chavasse, Puller, Boudinhon, De Clercq, Villien)[8] interprets the papal letter as referring to one anointing with blessed oil, which is the same as that prescribed by James. Even though this anointing is normally administered by priests and, on occasion, by bishops, it is also regularly done by the faithful. Thus the opposition that Innocent makes between "all Christians" and "priests" is not based on two different types of anointing but on that which exists between the whole and one of its parts. Innocent's specific use of the word "priests" (*sacerdotes*) indicates both priests and bishops, thereby avoiding any possible confusion that might arise from James's term "presbyter." These theologians conclude that, according to the Pope, if all the faithful can anoint, including the members of the hierarchical priesthood, surely the bishop is included. The limiting of the laity to anointing only themselves or members of their family is simply a statement of fact rather than a restriction imposed upon their faculty to anoint.

Moreover, these theologians note that Innocent attaches great importance to the consecrated oil. At the same time, they cannot find any evidence that the Pope implied that a distinction should be understood between the anointing with this oil as performed by priests and that by the faithful. Thus the lay anointing was understood to be sacramental.

The strength of this third opinion is that not only is it based on a grammatically accurate reading of the text, but it also appears to be the least forced of the three opinions. The obvious problem, however, is how to reconcile this interpretation with what is traditionally accepted today as the defined doctrine of the Church, which is that only a priest can be the valid minister of the sacramental anointing of the sick.

## The Testimony of Other Documents to the Anointing of the Sick in the Fifth to the Eighth Century

There are a number of other documents dating from the fifth to the eighth century that speak of the Church's practice of anointing the sick. While these documents are concerned primarily either with identifying this ritual with that prescribed in James 5:14-15 or with providing formulas for the blessing of the oil used to anoint the sick, several of these texts also shed some interesting light on the question of the minister of the anointing.

### *Specific references to the text of James*

The documents that more or less explicitly trace the roots of the Church's anointing of the sick to the words of James fall into four basic categories: Scripture commentaries on James 5:14-15, polemics against pagan practices, disciplinary decrees, and hagiographic accounts of the death of several saints.

1. *Scripture commentaries*

While the first full commentary on the Epistle of James dates from the mid-eighth century and is attributed to the Venerable Bede (d. 735),[9] some three centuries earlier Augustine, in his *De Scriptura Sacra speculum*, merely included the text of James 5:14-15 along with the rest of the chapter as part of the various prescriptions found in the New Testament pertaining to the living of a pious life.[10] The value of Augustine's testimony is that it substantiates that the ritual found in James was not peculiar to apostolic times but was a practice that had continued in the Church.

In the fifth century, Victor of Antioch, commenting on Mark 6:13, relates the Marcan text to James 5:14-15.[11] He attributes the effects obtained from the ritual prescribed by James to the prayer, while he views the oil as being simply a sign of them. Even though Victor clearly saw the two biblical references to anointing as being related, it is difficult to determine to what degree he understood the connection between the anointing performed by the Twelve and that called for in the Epistle.

The Venerable Bede, in commenting on Mark 6:13, also referred it to James 5:

> The Apostle James says: "Is anyone sick among you . . ." Thus it is evident from the Apostles themselves that this unction of holy Church was passed on so that those possessed or any other sick people were anointed with oil consecrated by pontifical blessing.[12]

By tracing an identification between the anointing in Mark with that of James and the eighth-century anointing of the sick by the Church, Bede established that the current practice of the Church actually dated back to the time of the Apostles.

At the same time, it should be noted that, unlike the biblical testimony, Bede held that this same anointing was to be used for the possessed, who appear to be a category of recipients different from "any other sick people." Furthermore, he insists on the episcopal consecration of the oil used for the anointing. Thus, even though Bede endeavored to identify the apostolic roots of the anointing of his day, it is clear that he did not take the Scripture references as the sole source for the ritual known to him.

In his commentary on James 5:14-15, Bede is principally concerned with those who are "infirm in body or in faith" who are to be anointed.[13] After recalling that there is often a cause-effect relationship between sin and sickness, he attributes the remission of the sick person's sins to confession rather than to the anointing. Referring to verse 16 of James, Bede makes the interesting observation that in the case of less serious sins, it is sufficient that the sick person confess them to another layperson. With more serious sins, however, the patient is bound by the "law of the priesthood" and must confess them to a priest.

On the basis of Bede's commentary on James 5:14-16, it would appear that he saw two rites identified there: a rite of anointing in the case of sickness, and a rite of penance, including a confession of faults, when the subject is in the state of sin. Bede, it seems, did not see the remission of sin as one of the effects of the anointing as it is found in James.

## 2. *Defense against pagan practices*

Cyril of Alexandria (d. 444) and the Armenian John Mandakuni (d. 498) both refer to the ritual prescribed by James in their polemic against those who were resorting to superstitious practices as cures for maladies.[14] Neither author comments on the Scripture passage, and about all that can be concluded from these two fifth-century documents is the presence of an institutional application of oil, based on the instruction of James, to which Christians were to have recourse in time of infirmity.

Caesarius, bishop of Arles (d. 543), wrote four sermons in which he, like Chrysostom and Mandakuni, encouraged the use of the Church's rite of anointing the sick in place of the pagan practices prevalent among many Christians at that time.[15] The essence of Caesarius' attack against the use of pagan practices by Christians is that even though they may benefit the body, they are harmful to the soul. What Caesarius prescribes is the reception of Communion and the anointing with oil as instructed by James. Implied in his argument is the recognition that the Christian can expect a twofold effect from this remedy of the Church. The fact that the healing of the body is one of these effects follows from Caesarius' insistence on the superiority of the Christian practice, which would be meaningless if the same effect that is often procured from the pagan rites could not be expected. In addition, Caesarius notes that the Christian receives from the anointing a spiritual effect, a healing of the soul and the forgiveness of sins. It is this unique characteristic that makes the Christian practice superior to those of the pagans, for the superstitious rites could only produce spiritual effects diametrically opposed to those received from the Church's remedy.

Caesarius is not clear as to whether these two effects are to be attributed to the anointing, to the Eucharist, or to both. From the texts of the four sermons, it would appear that bodily health stems from both. On the other hand, the forgiveness of sins seems to flow more from the anointing, which is the key to his argument on the superiority of the rite described by James.

Moreover, Caesarius does not specify the degree of seriousness of illness that merits this remedy of the Church. Throughout he speaks in terms of "any sickness," and his instructions indicate that the sick person is to "run to the church." To what degree this is meant to be taken figuratively cannot be determined from the sermons. What is clear, however, is that there is nothing in the words of Caesarius that would indicate that the Christian remedy is reserved only for serious illness or the danger of death.

The writings of St. Eligius (d. 660) are evidence that the problem of Christians resorting to pagan practices had not totally disappeared in the seventh century. In his sermon *De rectitudine catholicae conversationis*, Eligius enumerates a long list of practices from which Christians should abstain, among which is the use of superstitious incantations and rites in times of sickness. In place of these, he instructs that when "any infirmity" happens,

> let him who is sick confide in the mercy of God alone and receive with faith and devotion the Eucharist, the Body and Blood of Christ, and faithfully seek from the Church the blessed oil so that he may anoint his body in the name of Christ, and, according to the Apostle, "the prayer of faith will save the sick man and the Lord will raise him up" and he will receive not only health of the body but also of the soul, and there will be effected in him that which the Lord promised in the Gospel saying: "Whatever you ask for in prayer, believing, you will receive" (Matt 21:22).[16]

Thus, while Eligius instructs that Christians in times of illness should resort to the remedy of the Church as prescribed by James, he seems to attribute the effects of this remedy, the cure of both the body and the soul, to the prayer of faith rather than to the anointing.

### 3. *Disciplinary documents*

Among the canonical documents dating from this period and

referring to the Church's responsibility to the sick, many of those that speak of an anointing of the sick include a verbatim citation of chapter 8 of Pope Innocent's letter to Decentius, including the text from James therein.[17] These decrees understood this anointing to be the same as that prescribed by James and referred to by Innocent.

Specific mention should be made of the *De visitatione infirmorum*, which is frequently attributed to Augustine.[18] This text explicitly cites the reference from James 5, explains this anointing as a "typical unction of the Holy Spirit," and associates it with the administration of Viaticum. Caution must be exercised, however, in concluding on the basis of this document that the ritual presented in James had assumed, at the time of Augustine, a place among the "last rites" to be administered as a preparation for death. Most scholars agree that the *De visitatione infirmorum* originated from the end of the ninth century and has been falsely attributed to Augustine.

### 4. Hagiographic accounts

While not all the biographies of the saints originating from this period include detailed descriptions of their death, the majority that do so make no mention of their having received what are traditionally called the "last sacraments." At most, the accounts that speak of the death of the holy person make particular mention of his/her reception of the Eucharist, oftentimes calling it Viaticum.

There are, however, four saints of the sixth and seventh centuries whose biographies note that in their last moments they were anointed with holy oil, received Viaticum, and died shortly thereafter. While the accounts do not refer this anointing specifically to that of James, the wording is reminiscent of the biblical text.

St. Berlendus called in the priests and "asked for the holy oil; having received it, he consecrated his departure with the Body and Blood of the Redeemer." St. Eugene "called together the whole group of monks, and his venerable body was anointed with holy oil and his departure was accompanied by Viaticum." St. Cunegunda in a similar way called in the priests and "asked to be given the oil of anointing and Holy Communion." Finally, St. Tressan summoned the priests, confessed his faults, and "received the oil of sacred reconciliation . . . after which he asked for Viaticum."[19]

It should be recalled, however, that even though these saints died during this period, the accounts of their lives, at least in the case of Sts. Berlendus, Eugene, and Cunegunda, were not written until approximately three centuries later.[20] The dating of the *Life of St. Tressan* is disputed. Puller, an Anglican author, as well as Ruch, a more traditional Catholic commentator, both admit that this biography is probably of the ninth century.[21] As a result, these texts are not indicative of what the Church's understanding and practice of anointing were during the fifth to the eighth century.

*The consecrated oil*

It has already been noted that while there do not seem to have been any established rituals for the anointing of the sick during the first four centuries, the consecration of the oil used in this anointing was highly organized during this time. This same tendency seems to have continued during the centuries up to the Carolingian Reform. There is only one rite for anointing, that contained in the *Liber ordinum*, which most scholars agree dates from the eighth century. At the same time, there are a number of formulas for the blessing of oil that originate from the seventh century.

Among these prayers of blessing, the *Emitte* from the *Gelasian Sacramentary*, the second blessing of oil in the *Liber ordinum*, and three prayers from the *Bobbio Missal* all refer to both a spiritual and corporal effect from the use of this oil.[22] Clearly the oil in question is that used for the anointing of the sick.

The blessing *In tuo nomine*, also found in the *Liber ordinum*, appears to be Visigothic in origin.[23] This lengthy formula, which asks God to exorcise and sanctify the oil, contains the instruction from James 5. The oil is referred to as a remedy for a vast variety of maladies, the majority of which are physical in nature and considered to be the work of some demonic intervention. Consequently, the expulsion of these demons is also sought in the use of this oil.

It is interesting to note from this blessing that even though the prayer relates the use of the oil to the text of James, including the Apostle's words on the remission of sins, nowhere is this spiritual effect included in the rest of the formula. Whether the remission of sins was in fact expected from the use of the oil blessed by this formula cannot be determined.

## The minister of the anointing

The majority of documents dating from this period speak of the anointing of the sick as being sacerdotally administered. At the same time, however, there are a number of significant texts which, like the letter of Pope Innocent I, give the impression that this anointing was also performed by the laity.

In his commentary on James 5:14-15, the Venerable Bede interprets James's use of the term "presbyter" in the etymological sense as meaning "elder," and he seems to insist that those who intervene be older and not the young and less experienced. Furthermore, Bede states that more than one of the *seniores* are to be summoned. After describing the ritual anointing with consecrated oil accompanied by prayer, Bede quotes the letter of Innocent I:

> And not only is it allowed to presbyters, but, as Pope Innocent wrote, also to all Christians to use the same oil for anointing in their own need or that of their families, which oil is only to be confected by bishops.[24]

A number of questions arise from this interpretation of Bede. Did he understand "presbyter" as used by James in a broader sense as meaning more than "priest," and therefore cited the papal text as an authority to substantiate this interpretation? Or, if in fact he understood James as referring only to ordained priests, did he use the papal letter as an authority to legitimate the fact that lay Christians are permitted to anoint, even though James may have been silent on this?

If in the time of Bede only priests were the ministers of the anointing, his interpretation of "presbyter" as signifying "older" would be difficult to understand. Not only would he be discriminating against younger clergy, but also his insistence that "many presbyters" be called in, all of whom would be ordained and advanced in age and experience, would be hard to explain in the eighth century, when the local collegial presbyterate as a common phenomenon was a thing of the past. Such a restriction would appear to unduly limit the use of anointing.

While Bede's commentary is not conclusive evidence that the laity anointed in eighth-century England, there are strong reasons for presuming that this in fact was the case. Moreover, if Bede did recognize the practice of lay anointing, there is no evidence from the text to indicate that he distinguished between the anointing performed by the priests and that by the faithful. In fact, when he comments on James 5:16, he does make such a distinction when he refers to the confession of faults, which may be done to a lay person, while more serious sins must be confessed to a priest.

Caesarius of Arles makes some interesting but confusing comments regarding the minister of anointing. In two of his sermons it appears as though he is saying that in resorting to the remedy of the Church, the laity anointed themselves with the blessed oil. Sermon 50 states that when infirmity besets a person, he or she is to look for health

> from Christ, who is the true light; run to the church, anoint yourselves with blessed oil, receive the Eucharist of Christ. If you do these things, you will receive not only health of body but also of the soul.[25]

In Sermon 184 Caesarius writes:

> How much more correct and salutary it is that they would run to the church, receive the Body and Blood of Christ and faithfully anoint both themselves and their own with blessed oil, and, according to what the Apostles James says, they would receive not only health of body but also the remission of sin. For through him, the Holy Spirit has promised: "If anyone is sick . . . ."[26]

In his other two sermons, however, depending on how the Latin text is translated, Caesarius seems to say that this anointing is to be administered by the priest. Sermon 13 states:

> Whenever some infirmity happens, let him who is sick receive the Body and Blood of Christ; let him humbly and faithfully request the oil blessed by the priests [from the priests blessed oil], and then he may anoint [may be anointed] his body so that which is written will be fulfilled in him: "Is anyone sick among you . . . ."

The wording in Sermon 52 is almost identical.[27]

Thus it is not clear whether Caesarius considered it to be a normal procedure that the faithful applied the blessed oil to themselves in times of infirmity or that infirm Christians were to present themselves to be anointed by the priests.

The various opinions on this question follow substantially the same line of argumentation as the differing interpretations of the disputed passage in the letter of Innocent I. One school holds that the Latin verb *perungere* ("to anoint") is to be understood passively so as to mean that the "Christian is anointed by the priest with blessed oil." Thus the phrase "by the priests" modifies the verb and not the words *oleo benedicto* ("blessed oil").[28]

A second opinion resorts to the theory of the twofold usage of the same oil. If the faithful anointed themselves, as is implied grammatically by the text, it was a private or devotional use of the blessed oil. The fact that it was the priests who administered the sacramental anointing is inferred from the instruction that the sick person is to go to the church not only to be anointed but also to receive the Eucharist. Although not stated explicitly, it is understood that it was the accepted practice to receive the Eucharist from the priest. Therefore these authors presume that if it is the priest who administers the Eucharist to the infirm person, it is also the priest who prays over him or her and performs the anointing.[29] Moreover, this interpretation notes that since the time of Innocent, the oil used for anointing in the Western Church was blessed only by the bishop and not by priests. Consequently, the sermons can only be understood as saying that the faithful "are anointed by the priests with blessed oil."

A third opinion views these sermons as substantiating the fact of a lay anointing that would have been the same as that prescribed by James and therefore sacramental.[30]

For the most part, each of these opinions is subject to the same criticisms made above in the investigation of Innocent's letter. It must be noted, however, that the validity of the third opinion in this case rests to a great degree upon whether or not it was the practice, at least in the region with which Caesarius was familiar, to permit that the oil used for the anointing of the sick be blessed by priests.

Grammatically, the *De rectitudine catholicae conversationis* of Eligius implies that this oil was applied by the laity to themselves.[31] As was the case with the interpretations of both the text of Pope Innocent and the sermons of Caesarius, authors are divided as to whether the words of Eligius, "so that he may anoint his body," are to be understood in an active or passive sense.

Several commentators note that some manuscripts of this sermon have the passive form of the Latin verb, *ungatur*, instead of the active. Since the document states that this anointing is done "in the name of Christ," these authors see an explicit relationship to the words of James and therefore favor the passive form, indicating that the anointing is done to the sick person by the priests.[32] Those who read the text in an active sense and conclude that the sermon of Eligius is simply another indication of a lay administration of the anointing instructed by James support their opinion with the observation that the distinction Eligius makes between the seeking of the blessed oil from the Church and the anointing of the body would make no sense if it were the priests alone who performed the unction.

The prayer for the blessing of oil, *Emitte*, found in the *Gelasian Sacramentary* identifies three modes of administration: "anointing," "tasting," and "touching."[33] Since each of the Latin words used to indicate the method of use is in the active form, the question arises: Did those who received the oil blessed by this formula apply it to themselves in one of the three ways mentioned in order to receive the effects mentioned in the prayer? If this is so, would not the blessing *Emitte* be an indication that lay administration was practiced in the Church of the seventh and early eighth centuries at the time when the *Gelasian Sacramentary* was composed?

This same formula, although modified, is also found later in the *Gregorian Sacramentary*. One of the modifications in this version is the deletion of "tasting" as a mode of application. The other two forms of reception remain as in the original text of the prayer. Since the compiler of the *Gregorian Sacramentary* omitted "tasting" as a form of administration, perhaps because it was no longer in use at that time, would he not also have changed the other two verbs to the passive form if in fact the Church in Rome no longer permitted the faithful to apply this blessed oil to themselves? While this hypothesis is possible, it cannot be proved on the basis of the text of the blessing alone.

The one ritual for anointing that is generally accepted to originate from this period is entitled "An Order for Visiting or Anointing the Sick" and is found in the *Liber ordinum*.[34] From the contents of the ritual it is clear that it is to be carried out on the basis of what the Lord, after bestowing the Holy Spirit upon his disciples, commanded them to do. Even though it appears that the anointing is to be given to those who are seriously ill, the effects asked for in the prayers following the anointing emphasize recovery rather than preparation for death. Finally, it is explicitly stated that it is the priest who visits the sick and who is to administer the anointing and say the prayers.

## Observations

According to the numerous texts originating from the fifth to the eighth century which speak clearly of an anointing of the sick and relate it to the ritual prescribed in the Epistle of James, this anointing was administered for a variety of infirmities and in some cases even for the possessed. With the exception of the order for anointing found in the *Liber ordinum*, none of the documents indicate the degree of gravity that merits this unction, and nowhere is this ritual explicitly defined as being a preparation for death. On the contrary, the evidence dating from these centuries substantiates the conclusion that up to the time of the Carolingian Reform, Viaticum was understood to be the necessary sacrament for the dying.

By and large, during this period the anointing was considered to have both corporal and spiritual effects; and in several instances the forgiveness of sins was also specified. Apart from the sermons of Caesarius of Arles, the documents place equal if not greater emphasis on the corporal effects expected from the use of the anointing given in James. In those cases where demonic influence was considered to be the cause of the affliction, the texts usually imply the need for the removal of this influence as an effect so that the affliction can be remedied.

Regarding the oil used in the anointing, the texts almost universally refer to it as "sacred," "consecrated," "sanctified," and so on. As in the preceding period, the consecration of this oil continued to be highly organized. Depending on the reading of Sermons 13 and 52 of Caesarius, the documents all reserve the consecration of this oil to the bishop alone. The blessing of the oil was viewed as necessary in order to obtain the desired effects, even though James 5 makes no mention of the need for such a consecration. Moreover, according to several references, especially the letter of Innocent I, such great emphasis was placed on the consecration of the oil that it appears as though it was the consecrated oil that was regarded as the *sacramentum* rather than the application of the oil.

There is a great variety in the description of the modes of administering the blessed oil. Most often mentioned is the external use by anointing, although there is no apparent consistency as to what parts of the body were to be anointed. In addition, documents mention the "touching" of the oil as well as an internal use in the form of a drink. The anointing was usually accompanied by a "prayer," "prayer of faith," or the words "in the name of the Lord." The ritual found in the *Liber ordinum* designates an invocation of the Trinity. The general nature of the description of this prayer would indicate that during these centuries there was no fixed formula used for the anointing.

Finally, there seems to be overwhelming evidence to support the fact that lay anointing continued in the Church as an accepted practice up to the Carolingian Reform. While there are different schools of opinion that attempt to interpret this evidence, the primary texts appear to favor the opinion that admits the fact that historically the laity applied the blessed oil to themselves in times of sickness and also that this anointing was the same as that taught by James and was sacramental.

*Chapter Four*

# THE ANOINTING OF THE SICK FROM THE CAROLINGIAN REFORM TO THE MIDDLE AGES

The Carolingian Reform is generally accepted as having spanned the period from approximately 740 to 840. It was marked by the promulgation of numerous laws that attempted to regulate not only aspects of political and economic life but also Church discipline, liturgical practice, and popular piety. Among the decrees concerning ecclesiastical matters, many were aimed at correcting clerical corruption and negligence toward ministerial responsibilities.

The documents which originated from the late eighth century to the Middle Ages and which are concerned with the ministry to the sick fall into four basic categories: disciplinary texts, Scripture commentaries, hagiographic accounts, and liturgical rituals for anointing. Together they indicate a development in the Church's thinking regarding the purpose of the sacramental anointing of the sick, the mode of administering the sacrament, and the minister of this anointing.

## The Purpose of the Anointing of the Sick in this Period

The texts that date from these centuries are far from unanimous with regard to their testimony concerning the purpose of the sacramental anointing of the sick and the effects expected from it. In some cases they speak of a general twofold healing; in other instances greater emphasis is placed on the spiritual effects. Toward the end of this period, the anointing is spoken of more and more as a preparation for death.

*General healing*

There are a number of sources that continue to refer to the traditional twofold effect of spiritual and physical healing and imply that the anointing is to be administered to anyone who is sick. Among them, the *Statutes*, which have traditionally been attributed to St. Boniface, the archbishop of Mainz (d. 755), instruct priests to obtain the oil of the sick from the bishop and to remind the faithful to seek the anointing with this oil. The effects expected from this ritual are generally referred to as "being healed," and nothing is said regarding the severity of the illness warranting this ministry.[1]

In his commentary on Matthew 10:1, Rabanus Maurus identifies the anointing performed by the Apostles and that offered by the Church. Although the power of the Twelve to cure was a share in the power of Christ for the purpose of performing signs testifying to the kingdom and strengthening faith, Rabanus says, "Today, however, holy Church does spiritually what the Apostles did corporally. For she cures the sick with holy oil in the name of the Lord and at the same time prays for them to God that they may receive health."[2] Thus he speaks of this anointing in general terms as being "for the sick" for the purpose of receiving "health."

Likewise, Haymo of Halberstadt observes how the Apostles cured the sick, and then, reminiscent of Bede, he concludes, "Thus it is seen that this custom of the holy Church has been passed on from the Apostles that the sick be anointed with oil consecrated by a pontifical blessing."[3]

In the *Second Capitular* of Theodulf of Orléans, in addition to a detailed description of a Latin rite for administering extreme unction, there is also a Greek ritual for anointing the sick.[4] The formula used for the anointing according to the Greek practice bears a direct reference to James 5, and from the wording of the prayers it would appear that the Greek ritual was open to the likelihood of a physical healing.

The ancient Ambrosian rite for the anointing of the sick indicates several peculiarities in the way the sacrament was celebrated at this time in Northern Italy. Probably its most unique characteristic is that the oil used for the anointing is blessed by the priest at the time of administration. According to the various formulas used for this blessing, the effects intended from the application of the consecrated oil are twofold: "the health of mind and body," "strength of soul and body," "full safety."[5]

Similar to the Ambrosian rite, the Greek *Euchologion* also contains a blessing for the oil to be done by the priest at the time of administration. The prayer of blessing mentions both physical and spiritual healing. Moreover, during the actual anointings each of the seven priests who perform the ritual prays that God, with the intervention of all the saints, will "heal this servant from the infirmity of body that is detaining him and vivify him through the grace of Christ."[6] Thus, as in the Greek ritual found in the *Capitular*, the emphasis here seems to be placed on a bodily cure.

*Emphasis on spiritual effects and the remission of sins*

Among the early Celtic liturgies that contain a ritual for anointing the sick, the *Book of Dimma* and the *Book of Mulling*, both of which date from the ninth century, according to most scholars, and the *Stowe Missal* (9th–11th century) are of particular interest.[7] While the ritual from the *Book of Mulling* begins with several short prayers and an exhortation for the general spiritual and physical well-being of the sick person, in the other two rituals the spiritual effects appear to be given more prominence. The rite from the *Book of Dimma* clearly gives greater importance to the salvation of the soul, the remission of sins, and the conferral of grace, although the prayer that precedes the anointing does mention a cure of bodily infirmity. The *Ordo ad visitandum infirmum* from the *Stowe Missal* begins with a series of short prayers that mention a bodily cure but place the emphasis on the bestowal of grace, redemption, and the remission of sins.

The order for anointing found in the tenth-century *Codex Ratuldus* identifies the ritual with that prescribed by James. However, the effect mentioned in the formula that accompanies each of the eight anointings is the remission of sins. Three additional formulas emphasize the spiritual effects, although they do make a general reference to the sickness.[8]

In Book 1 of *De antiquis Ecclesiae ritibus*, edited by E. Martène, there are fourteen orders for anointing dating from these centuries.[9] Several of these orders (*IV, V, VI, VII*) contain traditional prayers that speak of a twofold effect expected from the anointing. However, from other prayers and especially the formula used to accompany the anointing, the principal effect sought seems to be the remission of sins. A further emphasis on the remission of sins is found in the fact that eight of the orders contain a general absolution of sins. Of these, *Orders IV, XI, XII, XIII,* and *XVII* include a specific reference to the power of binding and loosing.

In the "Order for the Visitation and the Anointing of the Sick" found in the English *Leofric Missal* (mid-11th century), there are a variety of forms to be used during the actual anointing. Some of them pray for the health of both the mind and the body, while others simply mention the remission of sins.[10]

*The anointing as a preparation for death*

In chapter 15 of Book 1 of the *Poenitentiale*, Egbert, the archbishop of York (732–767) refers to the anointing found in the Epistle of James and directs that when a person falls ill

> each one of the faithful, if he can, ought to receive this anointing, and the prescriptions which pertain to it, since it is written that anyone who avails himself of this custom, his soul shall be as pure after death as that of a child who dies immediately after baptism.[11]

This chapter is frequently cited in support of the Church's practice of anointing the dying in the eighth century because of the explicit mention of the fact that it cleanses the soul for immediate entrance into heaven. It should be noted, however, that in chapters 2, 3, and 10 of the *Poenitentiale*, which are concerned with the bestowal of penance at the time of death, mention is made of the "more ancient custom" of not denying Viaticum to the dying, but nothing is said of any ritual of anointing that is to accompany confession and the administration of the Eucharist.¹² Chapter 15 remains the sole place in which Egbert refers to the rite prescribed by James, and it is questionable whether it is accurate to see this document as an indication of a general practice in the Church.

Moreover, in a collection of canons which are attributed to Egbert and which govern the life and ministry of clerics regular, we read: "That according to the definition of the holy Fathers, if anyone is sick, let him be anointed diligently with sanctified oil and prayers by the priests."¹³ There is no reference here to the gravity of the illness, and nothing is said about the person's being at the point of death.

Halitgarius, the bishop of Cambrai (d. 831), writes of the anointing of the sick in chapter 16 of Book 3 of his *De poenitentia*. This chapter is located among those concerned with penance and Viaticum for the dying. Nevertheless, as was the case with the other documents mentioned above, the anointing is not specifically joined to these other ministrations as a preparation for death.¹⁴

In an epistle to all the faithful, Hincmar, archbishop of Rheims, does connect the anointing with penance and Viaticum as the ministry to the dying. He outlines the procedure of reconciliation for two individuals excommunicated because of the sin of incest. If they are in the danger of death and have resolved not to return to their relationships if they should recover, then he instructs: "Let them be reconciled by the priest, anointed with holy oil and be given the Body and Blood of Christ in communion."¹⁵ Likewise, in the latter half of the ninth century Riculf, bishop of Soissons, and Regino of Prüm both speak of the anointing of the sick and join it to the administration of penance and Communion, which is specifically referred to as Viaticum.¹⁶

It is in the descriptions of the death of the saints found in the hagiographic writings of this period that anointing is most clearly referred to as one of the "last rites" of the Church. In these accounts the anointing with holy oil is joined to the administration of Viaticum, usually in that order, on or near the day of death. Several of these texts expressly state that this anointing is administered according to the prescription of the Apostle James.¹⁷

As noted above, the *Second Capitular* of Theodulf of Orléans describes a ritual for administering extreme unction that was used in the Latin Church. In the opening instruction the *Capitular* states: "Priests are to be instructed regarding the anointing of the sick, penance, and Viaticum so that no one may die without Viaticum."[18] While the ritual does not specifically indicate the effects sought from the anointing, it would appear from the context of the instruction as well as the highly penitential tone of the rite that the remission of sins and the preparation for death are implied.

Finally, the ninth-century *Carolingian Order* for anointing, found in the *Gregorian Sacramentary*, contains prayers that ask for both physical and spiritual effects for the sick person, "whom weakness is moving to departure, and lack of strength is leading to death."[19] Even though a twofold effect is mentioned, this prayer from the *Carolingian Order* seems to indicate that the sick person is near death.

### Rituals for Anointing the Sick

Beginning with the time of the Carolingian Reform, a number of rituals for the anointing of the sick emerged. While the basic elements identified in James are found in all of them, the various rituals are extremely diverse in both their content and mode of celebration. The anointing was always done in conjunction with the celebration of the sacrament of penance or the giving of Communion or both. There was, however, variety with regard to the order in which these sacraments were administered. According to some rituals, the anointing preceded the reception of Communion, and there is no mention of the celebration of the sacrament of penance. Where the three sacraments were employed, the normal order was penance, anointing, and the Eucharist. The one exception to this is the ritual found in the *Book of Mulling*, where the anointing came before penance.[20]

There is no unanimity regarding the number of anointings to be performed or the parts of the body to be anointed. The Celtic liturgies do not seem to specify any particular anointings. In the other rituals the number varies from as few as five in the *Carolingian Order* and the *Roman Order X* to approximately fifteen anointings in the Latin order found in the *Second Capitular* of Theodulf.[21] The Greek *Euchologion* instructs that after seven anointings on the person who is sick, the "whole house" is to be anointed. This practice is unique to the *Euchologion*, and it is impossible to determine from the ritual its exact significance.[22]

Thus the ritual documents testify that there was no one set formula that was always used to accompany the sacramental anointing. They also contain a wide variety of prayers and readings. Among those that include passages from the Scriptures, the ritual from the *Book of Dimma* cites the words of Paul on the resurrection of the dead (1 Cor 15:19-22), and the order from the *Stowe Missal* has excerpts from Matthew on the teaching of Jesus about the resurrection and his second prophecy of the Last Times (22:23-33 and 24:29-31). These readings provide a context for perceiving how this sacrament was understood by those who celebrated the anointing with these rituals.[23] Only two of the rituals, those from the *Leofric Missal* and the Greek *Euchologion*, contain the traditional passage from James 5.[24]

There are a number of orders that call for the praying of the seven penitential psalms and the recitation of litanies as a penitential rite preceding the actual anointing. In some cases the Lord's Prayer is also included.[25] An additional penitential sign is found in those rituals that instruct that ashes be sprinkled on the person to be anointed.[26]

Among the most significant ritual variances is the use of the imposition of hands. In the majority of orders that incorporate this ritual gesture, it precedes the anointing and is clearly penitential in nature, frequently accompanying the praying of the penitential psalms and litanies.[27] The rubrics of the ritual found in the *Codex Titianus* call for a double imposition of hands—one at the beginning during the reception of reconciliation, and the other after the anointing but prior to the giving of the Eucharist.[28]

It was noted above that as the remission of sins became emphasized as an effect of the sacrament, a general absolution of sins began to be included in the ritual. This is found in eight of the orders collected by Martène. In two instances, *Orders XIII* and *XVII*, the absolution follows confession but precedes the anointing. In *Order XII* it comes after the anointing but before the giving of Communion, and in *Orders IV, VII, XI,* and *XV* the absolution follows the administration of all three sacraments and concludes the entire ritual.

An interesting rubric regarding the repetition of the sacrament is found in five of the rituals. The instruction in the *Carolingian Order* reads, "Let them do this for seven days, if there is the necessity, both Communion as well as the other duty; and the Lord will raise him up and if he be in sin, they will be remitted."[29]

The *Sacramentary of Rheims* is unique in that it contains an abbreviated order for use in the case of emergency. The shortened form includes a recitation of the Creed and a simple anointing with the form: "I anoint you with the blessed oil that you may be saved for all eternity in the name of the Father and of the Son and of the Holy Spirit." Then Communion is administered.[30]

Finally, it is evident from all the orders that they are administered by priests. Where they differ is in the number of priests who celebrate the ritual. In some cases the sacrament is administered by one priest, while in others the ritual is concelebrated by many priests. In several of these instances the rubrics direct that one priest anoints while another recites the accompanying prayer. Other rituals instruct that each of the priests is to anoint the sick person.[31]

The Greek *Euchologion* specifies that there are to be seven priests, each of whom blesses the oil to be used for the anointing, reads a passage from Scripture, recites several prayers of blessing, and anoints. They all use the same formula, beseeching God, with the intervention of all the saints, to "heal this servant from the infirmity of body which is detaining him and vivify him through the grace of Christ."[32] Following the anointings, all seven priests impose hands and pray for the forgiveness of the sick person's sins.

## The Minister of the Anointing

Like the liturgical documentation of this period, all the other primary sources are in agreement that the anointing of the sick was regularly administered by priests. There are, however, several texts that speak of the minister of anointing in a somewhat confusing fashion.

In his *Poenitentiale*, Egbert instructs that when a person falls ill, he is to call in

> his *priest* and *other ministers* of God so that *they* may admonish him, and the sick person may indicate to *him* his need and *they* may anoint him with holy oil in the name of the Lord; and through the prayers of the faithful and through the anointing, he may be saved and the Lord will raise him up, and if he be in sins, they will be remitted. . . .[33]

There is no doubt that Egbert identifies this anointing with that found in the Epistle of James, and that it is the function of the clergy to anoint. It is impossible to identify exactly who the "other ministers" mentioned by Egbert are.

Hincmar, the ninth-century archbishop of Rheims, in an instruction to his priests, reminds them to recall and to study the ritual of reconciling sinners and anointing the sick. He writes: "If the priest himself visits the sick, let him anoint [the sick] with holy oil and communicate [the patient] himself, not through anyone else."[34] This injunction appears to be an indirect reference to the fact that at some time someone other than priests anointed the sick and administered the Eucharist.

Another interesting comment is found in the commentary of Christianus Druthmar, a ninth-century monk of Corvey, who, in commenting on Matthew 10:1-16, relates Christ's election of the Twelve and their "ordination to be Apostles" to the seven grades of ministry in the Church. In an oblique reference to James, Druthmar speaks of the particular responsibility of deacons and priests to minister to the sick: "For it is the task of exorcists to cast out unclean spirits; it is of porters to have the powers of discretion; it is of deacons and priests to cure the sick, regarding whom, it is prescribed that they be brought in to the sick and anoint them."[35]

The question arises as to whether the Latin phrase for "regarding whom" (*de quibus*) refers to deacons and priests or simply to priests. The Latin construction is ambiguous, so it cannot be concluded with certitude that Druthmar clearly understood that deacons anointed the sick.

Three authors during this period cite the letter of Innocent I, but they significantly modify the papal text. In chapter 71 of his *Regula canonicorum*, Chrodegang, bishop of Metz (d. 766), speaks of the spiritual care of the sick, referring first to the text of James and then to the commentary of Innocent I. In the verbatim citation of the papal letter, he makes a significant grammatical change. Whereas the original controverted text contained the singular form *ungendum*, Chrodegang changes it to the plural form, *ungendis*.[36] The use of the plural seems to convey the more passive interpretation of Innocent's words, "The consecrated oil may be used for anointing not only priests but also all Christians," rather than the more active understanding that flows from the original singular, ". . . the use by priests and all Christians of this oil for anointing."

In his *De institutione laicali* (ca. 829), Jonas of Orléans condemns those Christians who in time of sickness resort to pagan rites rather than the anointing of the Church. He bases his instructions on Mark 6:13 and on Bede's commentary on James 5, which he quotes verbatim. In citing Bede, however, Jonas modifies Bede's reference to the disputed section of Innocent's letter regarding those who use the oil blessed by the bishop. Whereas Bede wrote, "It is permitted not only to priests, but also, as Pope Innocent has written, to all Christians to use this same oil for anointing in their own necessity or that of those close to them," Jonas writes, "It is permitted not only to priests, but as Pope Innocent has written, in the very same way it is also permitted that all Christians be anointed in their necessity."[37]

Jonas does not explain why he made this textual change. Even though he includes Bede's etymological interpretation of "presbyter" as signifying "elder," the whole thrust of Jonas' writing seems to emphasize the role of the priest to anoint. One possible explanation for the modification might very well be that lay anointing, which could be inferred from Innocent's words and which may have been in practice at the time Bede wrote, was now no longer permitted.

A similar tampering with the text of Innocent's letter is found in Book 3 of the *De poenitentia* of Halitgarius.[38] Once again, the hypothesis offered above to explain the modification in the *De institutione laicali* may apply here, and this may simply be another indication that any former practice of lay anointing had been discontinued and was no longer permitted.

## Observations

The documentary evidence of these centuries leads to a number of significant observations. First, as we have seen especially from the canonical and liturgical documents, the use of oil for anointing the sick was known throughout the Western and the Eastern Church at this time. However, as widespread as the use of this anointing may have been, there still was a need, especially in the Western Church, for disciplinary documents to encourage the use of this sacrament and also to regulate the priests regarding this ministry. This would appear to indicate that there was negligence, laxity, and abuse among both the laity and the clergy concerning extreme unction.

The first marked change from the tradition of the previous eight centuries is the relatively sudden rise of many orders for anointing, all of which were sacerdotally administered. In addition, the effects expected from this anointing moved from a more general reference to the twofold physical and spiritual healing to an emphasis on the spiritual effect, especially the remission of sins.

Although earlier documents frequently alluded to the connection between the administration of anointing and that of the Eucharist, more and more the texts of this period refer to this Communion as Viaticum. While Viaticum continued to be referred to as the sacrament of the dying, oftentimes, especially in many accounts of the death of saints, where the anointing was joined with Viaticum, it was considered to be one of the "last sacraments" administered as a preparation for death.

With regard to the orders for anointing, the predominant testimony is one of variety in content and construction. The rituals differ in the number of anointings, the places anointed, and the forms accompanying the anointings, as well as in the addition of such practices as readings from Scripture, the imposition of hands, the use of ashes, the recitation of the penitential psalms and litanies, the Creed, and the Lord's Prayer.

Furthermore, the documents all refer to the use of "blessed," "sanctified," or "consecrated" oil, which, generally speaking, was to be blessed by the bishop. Two exceptions to this are the ritual for anointing of the Ambrosian rite and the Greek *Euchologion*, both of which provide for the blessing of the oil by the priest prior to the anointing.

The fact that all the sources indicate that the anointing is to be performed by one or by several priests takes on special importance in the light of the absence of any reference to the practice of lay anointing, which was frequently attested to in the preceding eight centuries. Moreover, the grammatical tampering of the text of Innocent I's letter to Decentius in several instances, in an effort to give the controverted reference from the papal document a more passive interpretation, seems to substantiate the point that any practice of lay anointing was either non-existent or no longer permitted beginning with the Carolingian Reform.

The natural question that arises from all this evidence is: How does one explain all the changes in this sacrament, such as the shift in emphasis regarding the effect of the anointing, the location of anointing among the "last sacraments," and the restriction of its administration to priests? There is a certain logic to the conclusion that the large number of disciplinary reforms, enacted at this time to correct the abuses and negligences of the priestly ministry, would have in some way directly influenced the restricting of the administration of this anointing to priests.

As a further explanation for these changes, many scholars point to the prevalence at this time of the practice of "deathbed penance."[39] According to this opinion, penance in the earlier centuries had a predominantly public form. Because of the strenuousness of this practice, the faithful frequently delayed the reception of penance until they were near death. At the time of the Carolingian Reform, deathbed penance was extensively practiced and was administered only by the priests. The proponents of this theory suggest that with the renewed interest in the anointing of the sick, a practice apparently also neglected by the faithful, this ministry to the sick became associated with deathbed penance, resulting both in the emphasis on its being a preparation for death and in its administration being solely the responsibility of priests.

In a variation on this theory, Poschmann supports the hypothesis by noting that the penance of the sick was considered a form of public penance that carried with it heavy obligations if the person should recover. As a result, when the practice of anointing was encouraged again, it became associated with the ministry to the dying, which was the duty of the priest.

Regardless of the accuracy of these opinions, the documents of this period of history clearly indicate the fact of distinct changes regarding the anointing of the sick beginning with the time of the Carolingian Reform. These developments mark a significant turning point in the Church's understanding and practice of the sacrament of extreme unction.

*Chapter Five*

# THE ANOINTING OF THE SICK FROM THE MIDDLE AGES TO THE SIXTEENTH CENTURY

In the preceding chapter it was seen that, beginning with the time of the Carolingian Reform, there were a number of distinct changes in the Church's understanding of the anointing of the sick. These developments not only continued on through the Middle Ages up to the sixteenth century, but they became more systematized and uniform in both the theological teaching and liturgical practice of the Church.

## The Scholastic Theologians

The numerous theological treatises on extreme unction written in the Middle Ages dealt not only with the institution and sacramentality of anointing but also with the specific questions of the effects of the sacrament, the proper subject and minister of anointing, and the use of consecrated oil.

*The early Scholastic period*

In the *Epitome theologiae Christianae*, which has been attributed to Peter Abelard, extreme unction is accepted as a sacrament, the principal effect of which is the remission of sins. This anointing is understood to be a preparation for death. "Truly this sacrament is the last and quasi-consummation of them all . . . which is to be bestowed at the time of death where either all sins, if there are any, or the greatest part of them are forgiven."[1] When discussing the possibility of the repeated reception of extreme unction, Abelard concluded in the affirmative, making the interesting observation that it is not one of the "major sacraments."

Hugh of St. Victor, in his treatise *De sacramentis*, admitted the possibility of a twofold effect of this anointing, although he recognized that a bodily cure may not always be expedient for the soul. Tracing what appears to be a cause/effect relationship between the remission of sins and physical healing, he noted: "In order to obtain the health of the body, the soul is first to be cured. And if by chance, the body does not return to pristine health, there is no danger if only the soul receives back its health."[2] The possibility of a twofold effect surfaced again when Hugh discussed whether or not extreme unction can be repeated. He affirmed that it can because "he who is anointed with oil is anointed so that sins be forgiven him and infirmity alleviated. But he who is justified can sin again, and he who is cured can fall sick again."[3]

When discussing the same question in the *Summa sententiarum*, Hugh made an interesting observation regarding the matter of extreme unction, the episcopally consecrated oil: "When it is said that a sacrament is not to be repeated, it is not to be understood of the sacrament according to its part but according to its whole." After explaining this distinction by using the analogy of baptismal water, which is blessed only once even though it may be used many times, he concluded: "The repetition [of extreme unction] is licit with regard to the person who receives the sacrament again; however, because the same host is not blessed again or the same oil, the sacrament is not repeated."[4] It would appear that Hugh of St. Victor was sympathetic to an opinion that viewed the consecrated oil as a sacrament.

Peter Lombard began his treatment of extreme unction in the fourth book of his *Sentences* by stating: "The anointing of the sick is done *in extremis* with oil consecrated by a bishop."[5] Lombard noted the twofold effect of extreme unction and the conditional nature of the physical healing. Relying on Hugh of St. Victor, he distinguished between the *sacramentum* of extreme unction, which is the exterior anointing, and the *res sacramenti*, the interior anointing, which effects "the remission of sin and the increase of virtue."[6]

When discussing whether the sacrament can be repeated, Lombard commented on the consecrated oil used in the anointing: "Just as the body of Christ cannot be received except of consecrated bread, nor can this anointing be done except from oil consecrated by a bishop; thus this consecration seems to pertain to the power of the sacrament."[7] Thus Lombard held that only oil consecrated by a bishop would be the valid matter for the administration of extreme unction.

*The Dominican School—Albert the Great and Thomas Aquinas*

In the opinion of both Albert the Great and Thomas Aquinas, the sacramentality of extreme unction flowed not only from its divine origin but also from the fact that it is a sign especially productive of spiritual effects. For Albert, extreme unction is that sacrament "made from an anointing with consecrated oil, conferring on the sick the remedy against the *reliquia peccati* ["remnants of sin"], and if it is expedient, the alleviation of the infirmity of the body."[8] He explained these "remnants of sin" as being "that disease of spiritual infirmity remaining from original sin and actual sins."[9] Albert likewise traced a cause/effect relationship between the infirmity of the soul and that of the body. Consequently, an alleviation of the spiritual disease can effect that of the physical order, although he admitted that any bodily cure is only secondary and need not always follow.

According to Thomas Aquinas' general understanding of the sacraments, each of the sacraments has one principal effect. In the *Contra gentiles* he writes: "This sacrament is ordered against the infirmity of the body insofar as it follows from sin; however, it is clear that this sacrament is ordered against the consequences of sin."[10] Thus he considered the removal of the remnants of sin to be the effect unique to extreme unction. By removing those defects by which man is spiritually infirm and which impede the soul from the perception of glory, Aquinas concluded that "this sacrament is the ultimate remedy that the Church can confer, quasi immediately disposing the soul to glory."[11] Thomas admitted that sins may be remitted as a result of the reception of anointing, but only indirectly. In other words, since the strength brought by the grace given in this sacrament is not compatible with sin, "*ex consequenti*, if sin is found, either mortal or venial *quoad culpam*, it removes it."[12]

Thomas insisted on retaining the dimension of a physical cure principally because of his notion that sacraments effect by signifying. Therefore, since extreme unction is in the form of a medicine, and the purpose of medicine is to remove illness, this sacrament "signifies and causes the spiritual cure through the corporal cure that it effects exteriorly."[13] Nevertheless, he recognized, as did Albert, that a physical healing follows only when it is expedient for the spiritual cure, and as such it remains only a secondary effect.

The position of both Albert and Thomas on the effects of extreme unction logically led to their conclusions regarding the subject of this sacrament. First of all, extreme unction can only be given to the sick and not to the well.[14] Moreover, they both insisted not just that the subject be sick, but because extreme unction is a remedy removing any impediments to an immediate entrance into glory, the patient must be in the danger of death. They also held that children cannot receive extreme unction. The only remnants of sin that children can have are those of original sin. According to the Dominicans, however, extreme unction is directed against the remnants of actual sins, of which children cannot be accused, and those of original sin only insofar as they have been strengthened through actual sin. Finally, for both theologians, this sacrament is not to be administered to the mentally incompetent.[15]

Albert did not specifically address the question of the minister of extreme unction, but Thomas posed the question of whether or not a lay person can administer the anointing. His two principal arguments against lay anointing were, first, "In this sacrament there is the remission of sins. But the laity do not have the power of remitting sins. *Ergo*."[16] Second, because extreme unction is administered in the name of the whole Church, it can only be done by a public person of the Church. Since, according to Thomas, a lay person is a private person, he/she cannot be permitted to administer the anointing.

With regard to whether a deacon can anoint, Thomas recalled that James instructed that "the presbyters of the Church be brought in," and Thomas observed that "deacons have only purgative power, not illuminative. Since illumination is given through grace, a deacon cannot *ex officio* give any sacrament in which grace is conferred; therefore, neither this one, since grace is conferred in it."[17]

In determining the matter of extreme unction, both Albert and Thomas agreed that consecrated oil is of the essence of this sacrament. While they insisted that this consecration is to be performed only by a bishop, Thomas refuted the opinion which held that the sacrament is in the episcopal blessing of the oil. Arguing that the only sacrament where the blessing of an element brings the sacrament into being is the Eucharist, he concluded that "this sacrament [extreme unction] consists in the anointing itself . . . and the matter of this sacrament is the sanctified oil."[18]

### The Franciscan School—Alexander of Hales and Bonaventure

Like the Dominicans, the Franciscans accepted the sacramentality of extreme unction, which is to be administered *in extremis* with a view to preparing a dying person for entrance into heaven, but they disagreed on precisely how this sacrament is a preparation for death. Both Alexander of Hales and Bonaventure were of the opinion that extreme unction not only removed the *reliquiae peccati* ("remnants of sin"), but it is also directed against the disease of sin. They held that, while other sacraments are related to original sin and mortal sin, extreme unction remitted principally those venial sins which, as Bonaventure qualified, are not found *in statu viae* ("during one's lifetime") but *in statu egrediendi* ("at the time of death").[19] Observing that venial sins weigh the soul down, Bonaventure concluded that through extreme unction the soul is elevated by devotion, it receives vigor, and as a consequence there is a repression of corporal annoyances.

Both Franciscans agreed with Albert and Thomas that extreme unction is to be administered only to a person seriously ill and in danger of death. They likewise rejected its being given to children or to the mentally incompetent.[20]

With regard to the minister of anointing, Alexander recognized the sacerdotal administration of extreme unction in saying that "the anointing, which is made with oil on the sick by the priest whose duty it is, with the intention of doing what the Church does and with a prayer of faith, is a sacrament."[21] Bonaventure's reasoning for sacerdotal administration centered principally around two arguments: first, because the matter of the sacrament is consecrated, the minister should have consecrated hands; second, the duty of praying for others in the Church belongs to the priest.[22]

While Alexander merely stated that the matter of the sacrament is the oil of the sick, Bonaventure was more precise. For him, it is oil consecrated by a bishop; and his position was based on a rather unique theory regarding the institution of extreme unction:

> The Holy Spirit instituted this sacrament through the Apostles, who could not sanctify except through God: therefore, the matter is not a simple element but oil consecrated through the word of the bishops, who are the successors of the Apostles, and as the Holy Spirit instituted it through the Apostles, so even now the consecration is done through bishops.[23]

At the same time, in light of the traditional Scholastic theory regarding the essential components of a sacrament, Bonaventure refuted the opinion of those who viewed the consecrated oil to be the sacrament: "The oil has neither perfect signification nor sanctification until it is applied to the sick and accompanied by the sacerdotal prayer; then there is signified the grace that anoints internally and only then is there the sacrament, not before."[24]

*Other Medievalists*

There are a number of other medieval theologians who, while they are not as well known as the famous Dominicans and Franciscans, made a number of interesting observations regarding the effects of the sacrament of extreme unction and the proper matter and minister of the anointing.

### 1. Gerald of Cambrai (1146-1220)

In his *Gemma ecclesiastica*, Gerald of Cambrai responded to the question of whether the Eucharist or extreme unction can be administered by a lay person. Noting that this practice had in fact gone on and had been prohibited by a number of synods as an abuse, he says: "This is to be so understood unless there is unusual necessity, because then if the priest, by chance, cannot do it himself, this office can be fulfilled by a deacon or even a layman; just as the duty of baptizing, so too, that of the extreme unction of the sick."[25] To support his position, Gerald first cited Isidore, who had written with regard to baptism: "It is sure that baptism is to be conferred only by priests; it is not licit for deacons to fulfill this ministry without a bishop or priest unless they are without a doubt absent and the danger of death is imminent; then it is even permitted to the faithful laity." His second source was the celebrated text from the letter of Pope Innocent to Decentius, which Gerald accurately quoted verbatim.[26]

### 2. Pope Innocent V (Peter of Tarantaise, 1225-1276)

According to Pope Innocent V, the principal effect of extreme unction was the remission of venial sins specifically for the purpose of making people more worthy to enter into glory. Since only the priest can forgive sins, and because the prayer here is the public prayer of the Church, Innocent insisted on the sacerdotal administration of extreme unction.[27]

Perhaps the most interesting aspect of Innocent's treatment of anointing was his response to the opinion that regarded the consecrated oil as the sacrament. Through the use of a distinction, he seemed to strike a compromise position:

> The sacrament is the material element, as Hugh of St. Victor says; the anointing itself is not the material element, but the oil; therefore the anointing is not the sacrament . . . a sacrament can be predicated of something in two ways, either *per causam*—thus the

oil can be called a sacrament—or *per essentiam*—then the anointing is the sacrament.[28]

### 3. Duns Scotus

Continuing the basic position of Alexander of Hales and Bonaventure, Duns Scotus held that the primary purpose of extreme unction was to remove venial sins insofar as they are an impediment to one's entrance into glory. Thus he likewise concluded that this anointing can be administered only to those who are seriously ill and in danger of death. Furthermore, he too was of the opinion that, as was determined by James, only priests can anoint.[29]

### 4. Thomas Waldensis (d. 1430)

Thomas Waldensis defended extreme unction against the attacks of Wycliff. The basis of Thomas' argument regarding the origin of this sacrament was drawn from Bede's commentaries on Mark 6:13 and James 5:14-16. When discussing the minister of anointing, he quoted Bede's reference to Innocent I's letter and observed:

> . . . according to Innocent, that this is permitted not only to priests but also to all Christians, he means where the supply of priests is altogether lacking; just as in the case of extreme necessity, it is licit for any Christian to baptize. Otherwise, the mandate of the Apostle ought to be observed that the priests be brought in.[30]

Thomas did not use Bede as an authority to establish lay anointing as a historically common phenomenon in earlier times but only as a possibility in the case of an emergency, as was the accepted practice with baptism. Although he clearly restricted this exercise of lay anointing, there is no doubt about the fact that he considered this administration to be sacramental.

### 5. Simeon of Thessalonica

Perhaps the most frequently quoted Eastern theologian of the Middle Ages on matters regarding extreme unction is Simeon of Thessalonica. According to him, this sacrament has both the physical effect of healing and the spiritual effect of the forgiveness of sins. Simeon openly spoke out against the practice of the Latin Church of administering this sacrament to the dying:

But the Latins with all their innovating have adulterated the doctrine of this mystery, and they say it is not to be given to the sick but to the dying because it forgives sin but fails to assist with the restoration of health."[31]

For Simeon, the anointing of the sick is a sacrament for the living, to be administered as a cure that the sick may live and remain cleansed from sin. By conferring it only on those who no longer can expect health, he concluded that the Latin Church had gone against apostolic tradition.

Moreover, Simeon held that the ritual of anointing was to be administered by priests. In fact, he insisted on the presence of seven priests, although he admitted that in the case of necessity the minimum number could be three. In no way could he accept that only one priest could confer this anointing. Furthermore, as was found with the Greek *Euchologion*, he directed that the priests bless the oil before administering it.

### Disciplinary and Conciliar Documents

The disciplinary and conciliar documents of this period fall into two general classifications: those principally concerned with the practice and administration of the sacrament, and those professions of faith that accept extreme unction as one of the sacraments of the Church.

#### 1. *The practice of the sacrament*

There are a number of disciplinary documents that date from this period, some of which reminded priests of their responsibility to administer the sacrament of anointing to the sick.[32] Others referred to the apparent abuse by priests of demanding high stipends for this ministry, and they forbade the reception of any recompense for administering extreme unction.[33] In some places the negligence of the priests in this regard must have been so great that severe censures were prescribed for those who failed in this responsibility. The Synod of Evreux (1287) decreed:

> If anyone, young or old, because of the fault, negligence, or absence of his priest dies without baptism, confession, reception of the Body

of the Lord, and extreme unction, the priest so convicted is to be suspended from the celebration of the divine mysteries, which suspension is not to be lifted until he has won expiation by a penance worthy of so great a crime.[34]

Still other documents indicate that many of the faithful continued to be lax with regard to the reception of this sacrament. In addition to their turning to superstitious practices, another apparent explanation for this neglect was their misconception of the obligations they would be required to assume if they recovered, such as abstaining from eating meat, from legitimate sexual intercourse, and from walking barefoot. The fact that these misconceptions continued through the Middle Ages is substantiated by those texts which, while noting that this sacrament could be repeated if the danger of death arose again, also instructed priests to inform the people that if they recovered, they were not bound to such false obligations.[35]

Among these conciliar and synodal decrees, there are some that identified the effects of the anointing as being primarily spiritual, in particular the remission of sins. When they mentioned physical healing, it was always in a secondary fashion and only on the condition that it was expedient that the sick person recover.[36] By the time of the sixteenth century, however, the majority of these documents clearly referred to extreme unction as a preparation for death.[37]

## 2. Professions of faith

There are several professions of faith that were prescribed for both schismatic groups and individuals who had strayed from the official teaching of the Church. These professions included an acceptance of each of the sacraments, including extreme unction.[38] The bull *Inter cunctas* of Martin V (February 22, 1418) states that all who condemn the reception of the sacraments of confirmation, extreme unction, and the solemnization of matrimony sin grievously (DS 1259).

Undoubtedly the most important profession of faith prior to the Council of Trent regarding extreme unction is found in the *Decretum pro Armenis* of Eugene IV (November 22, 1439) at the Council of Florence (DS 1324-25). Its significance stems not only from the comprehensiveness of its content but also from the fact that the decree was frequently referred to by the Tridentine Fathers. With regard to extreme unction, the decree identifies the matter and the form of the sacrament and states that it is to be administered only to those sick persons who are in the danger of death. Moreover, it states that the minister of the anointing is the priest and notes that the effects of the sacrament are the healing of the soul and of the body, but only insofar as it is beneficial to the person. Although the text of the decree contains the traditional passage from James 5, it does not include the remission of sins among the effects.

## Liturgical Documentation

The proliferation of orders for the anointing of the sick that began with the time of the Carolingian Reform continued through the Middle Ages up to the sixteenth century. While these rituals have many things in common, there are a number of ways in which they differ from one another.[39]

### Orders for anointing used in the Latin Church of the Middle Ages

Among the various elements that all these medieval rituals have in common is the fact that they are all sacerdotally administered. They all refer to the use of "sacred" or "sanctified" oil, which in some orders is given the specific name "the oil of the sick." While the majority of the rituals use the general Latin terms for "sick" (*infirmus* or *aegrotus*) to identify the subject, there are several orders that specifically determine the condition of the sick person as being *in extremis* and approaching death.[40]

The effects intended from the anointing as indicated in the prayers are generally twofold, although the spiritual effect, especially the remission of sins, is emphasized. In some cases the form that accompanied the actual act of anointing mentions only the forgiveness of sins. Like several rituals from the preceding period, a number of orders include a general absolution of sins. Furthermore, most of the rituals direct that penance and Eucharist accompany the administration of anointing, although they differ regarding the order in which the three sacraments are to be given.

The principal differences between the orders concern the number of anointings called for and the parts of the body to be anointed. Even at this relatively late date, there still was not a designated form that was universally used by all the different rituals. Other elements found in some rituals and not in others include a blessing with ashes, the imposition of hands, the praying of the penitential psalms and litanies, and the incorporation of the Lord's Prayer and a profession of faith.

*Oriental rituals for anointing the sick*

Several Oriental rituals for the anointing of the sick provide an insight into how this sacrament was understood in the Eastern Churches during these centuries.[41] From the tone of the prayers found in them, it appears that in the East this sacrament was intended more for the sick, with a greater emphasis placed on bodily health than in the West.

The Eastern ritual was normally concelebrated by seven priests, each of whom performed the anointing. Common to almost all the orders is the provision for the blessing of the oil by the priests at the time of administration, although some of the Churches, especially those that were reunited with Rome, also acknowledged the prerogative of the patriarch and the bishops to consecrate the oil on Holy Thursday. In some instances the orders actually provide two rites for blessing—one for the patriarch, the other for ordinary priests. Several rituals direct that after the sick person has been anointed, the ministers celebrating the sacrament are to be anointed with this same oil. In addition, as was found in the Greek *Euchologion*, the bystanders were also anointed sometimes.

Other elements common to many of the Oriental rites include the imposition of the Gospel book on the head of the patient, the recitation of the Creed, the imposition of hands by the priests, and the administration of confession and Communion, although here too the order of the three sacraments is not always the same.

With the separation of many of the Eastern Churches from Rome, the practice of anointing the sick tended to fall into disuse in the East. The most common procedure among those Churches that reunited with Rome was to adopt the Roman ritual, translating it into their respective vernaculars.[42] Although, by and large, the provision for the concelebration of the sacrament was maintained by the uniates, the blessing of oil became reserved more to the patriarch and bishops.

*Sixteenth-century orders for anointing*

In his extensive treatise on extreme unction, the eighteenth-century theologian Jean Launoy included a listing of orders for the purpose of demonstrating the gradual development and change regarding the sacramental form used for anointing. Among them are a number that date from the first half of the sixteenth century; they are of particular interest because they reflect how the sacrament of extreme unction was understood and celebrated at the time of the Reformation and the Council of Trent.[43]

According to the rubrics of these rituals, extreme unction was to be administered principally to the seriously ill who were in the danger of death. Their instruction that the sick person confess and be absolved and the inclusion in each ritual of a general absolution with a special view to eternal life make it clear that the primary purpose of these rites was the remission of sins in preparation for entrance into future life. It is evident, therefore, that by the sixteenth century, at least in the Churches in which these rituals were used, extreme unction had assumed a definite place as part of the final preparation of a person for death.

## Observations

The development of Scholastic sacramental theology during the Middle Ages had a profound effect on the Church's theological understanding of extreme unction. According to the medievalists, the sacraments are primarily a means of grace. Thus the spiritual effect of anointing became primary, and physical healing assumed a secondary and conditional role. Given the Scholastics' continued emphasis on the spiritual nature of the effects of this sacrament, extreme unction eventually reached the point of being a preparation for death. Although there were two different schools of thought as to precisely how the sacrament prepared a person to enter into eternal life, the medieval theologians were in agreement on the nature of extreme unction, which explained why it was to be administered only to those who were seriously ill and in danger of death.

Furthermore, all the Scholastics taught that, as was the Latin custom, only oil consecrated by a bishop was to be used for the anointing. This episcopal consecration was of such significance that it was viewed as being required for the valid administration of the sacrament. While the major theologians rejected the opinion that tended to view the consecrated oil as a sacrament, others such as Hugh of St. Victor and Pope Innocent V attempted to demonstrate in what sense the blessed oil could be termed a "sacrament."

All the medievalists were in agreement that the minister of the anointing was the priest. The reasons most often cited for sacerdotal administration included the fact that the sacrament remitted sins, which only priests can do; the consecrated matter demanded a consecrated minister; and finally, since the prayer of the sacrament is public and done in the person of the Church, it can only be performed by a public ecclesiastic, the priest. Where there were references to a lay anointing, as in the writings of Gerald of Cambrai and Thomas Waldensis, this possibility was recognized not as a regular phenomenon but only as an exception in the case of necessity.

With regard to the practice of extreme unction during this period, the disciplinary, creedal, and liturgical documents demonstrate that many of the trends and attitudes that began to appear at the time of the Carolingian Reform continued in the Church of the Middle Ages, became more widespread, and in time were institutionalized. In addition, a number of these texts indicate not only that the abuses and negligences of the preceding centuries had extended into the Middle Ages, but also that the acceptance of extreme unction as a sacrament had become a point of disagreement for those who had separated themselves from the Church.

Even though anointing was accompanied by Viaticum, the order for administering the sacraments had become inverted, so that the anointing was conferred last. The rite was normally concluded with a general absolution to ensure immediate entrance into glory. Consequently, with the possible exception of the Eastern Churches, by the sixteenth century extreme unction had become, pastorally and liturgically, not just one of the "last rites" of the Church but the sacrament that prepared a person for death.

While the many rituals dating from this period continued to retain the characteristic of variety in their contents and mode of celebration, they all were to be sacerdotally administered. Furthermore, although some of the Oriental orders retained the practice of having the priests bless the oil before administering it, in the Latin Church the rituals all called for oil consecrated by a bishop.

As one looks back over the first sixteen centuries of the history of this sacrament, it is evident that, beginning with the time of the Carolingian Reform, there were significant changes in the way extreme unction was understood and practiced. Whereas prior to the eighth century the anointing was clearly to be administered to the sick in general, with the expectation that a physical cure was as important an effect as a spiritual healing, by the time of the Reformation it had become "extreme unction," given only to the dying. Moreover, after eight centuries, during which period there was no organized manner for celebrating the sacrament, numerous rituals began to emerge. At the same time the administration of anointing was restricted solely to priests, resulting in the consequent disappearance of what had been the widespread practice of lay anointing. In view of all these changes, the question arises: Were these developments simply the emergence in time of aspects of divine revelation concerning this sacrament, aspects which, though hidden sometimes for as long as eight centuries, were present from the very beginning and which pertain to the nature of extreme unction?

There are a number of factors that make it difficult to give an affirmative answer to this question. First of all, these changes were of a radical nature and did not affect simply secondary aspects of the sacrament. Second, even with these changes there was great divergence within the universal Church with regard to the way extreme unction was both understood and liturgically administered. These differences existed not only between the Church in the West and that in the East, but even within the Western Church. Third, the exercise of the disciplinary function of the Church was noted not only in the correction of abuses and negligences among both clergy and laity regarding the anointing of the sick, but also in determining the sacramental form for anointing and the composition of the rituals with which it was to be administered. There was also the Church's insistence on the use of episcopally consecrated oil, a practice neither universally taught nor followed. Finally, the restricting of the anointing of the sick to priests, accompanied by the sudden cessation of lay anointing, happened at a time of great clerical reform.

This last factor is of special significance when it is recalled that numerous documents of the first eight centuries of the Church seem to support the opinion that in the consciousness of the Church of that time, the practice of lay anointing was regarded as being sacramental. When the sources of later centuries refer to lay anointing, they speak of a limited practice permissible only in cases of extreme emergency. Morever, in an effort to substantiate sacerdotal administration, numerous documents of later tradition either grammatically tampered with, or attempted to give a forced interpretation to, the letter of Pope Innocent I, which, prior to the Carolingian Reform, was frequently cited as authenticating the practice of lay anointing. All this evidence proves the hypothesis that the restricting of this anointing to priests was not the universal practice throughout the history of the Church.

It appears much more probable that these developments regarding extreme unction, including the restricting of its administration solely to priests, were not so much a continuation of what was determined by Christ or the Apostles, but were in fact examples of the Church either specifying what divine revelation had left undifferentiated or in some way recognizing its authority over this anointing, giving concrete form to various aspects of the sacrament as historical circumstances arose. These particular determinations, even though not specified by divine revelation, would have been binding for the Church at that time for the valid administration of the sacramental anointing of the sick. Consequently, the history of the development of extreme unction and the more theological question regarding the nature of the changes in the sacrament provide an invaluable foundation for understanding and evaluating both the teaching of the Reformers and the response of the Council of Trent concerning the sacrament of anointing, especially canon 4 regarding its minister.

*Chapter Six*

# THE TEACHING OF THE PROTESTANT REFORMERS ON THE SACRAMENT OF EXTREME UNCTION

Volumes have been written on the political, social, economic, ecclesiastical, and theological influences that gave rise to the movement now known as the sixteenth-century Protestant Reformation. What began principally as a reaction to both historical abuses and inadequate and often misleading theological teaching gave birth to dogmatic differences that for centuries have resulted in the scandalous division of Christianity.

Repeatedly during this period the Protestant Reformers requested the opportunity to appear before a general council of the Church in the hope that controverted theological positions could be reconciled. It was not until approximately thirty years after Martin Luther posted his famous *Ninety-five Theses* on the cathedral door at Wittenberg that a general council was called at Trent; however, only bishops in communion with Rome were summoned. Although Trent viewed itself as a reforming council, and in fact did much to correct disciplinary and ecclesiastical abuses prevalent at that time, the Reformers could not acknowledge this council. The die had been cast, and Trent set about its principal task of restating Catholic doctrine as a polemical enterprise against the writings of the Reformers.

With regard to the response of Trent to the Reformers' position on the minister of extreme unction, it must be noted from the outset that the writings of the Protestants contain only a minimal systematic treatment of this sacrament and even less concerning the proper minister of the anointing of the sick. Thus the Reformers' theology on extreme unction must be seen in light of their teaching on the sacraments in general, especially the questions of sacramental institution and the minister of the sacraments.

## The Institution and Number of the Sacraments

The sacramental theology of the Reformers was a logical consequence of their doctrine on justification and the unique authority attributed to the recorded Word of God in the Scriptures. Recalling the fact that God has made the promise of justification, the fundamental task of the human person is to place one's faith in the Word of God, which speaks of this promise realized in Christ and to which promise God is always faithful. According to the Reformers, this Word of God is encountered in the Scriptures and, as directed by the Scriptures, in the sacraments. Article 1 of the *Geneva Confession* of 1536 states:

> First we affirm that we desire to follow Scripture alone as the rule of faith and religion without mixing with it any other things which might be devised by the opinion of men apart from the Word of God and without wishing to accept for our spiritual government any other doctrine than what is conveyed to us by the same Word without addition or diminution, according to the command of our Lord.[1]

The basic Reformation concept of a sacrament was an external sign instituted by Christ to which a divine promise of grace had been affixed for the purpose of supporting and confirming one's faith in that promise. The *Confessio Augustana* notes:

> The sacraments were instituted not only that they be marks of public acknowledgment among men, but more that they be presented as signs and testimonies of God's will toward us for the purpose of stirring up and confirming faith in those who use them.[2]

Given the function of the sacraments as described above, the Reformers emphasized that it is only through the act of faith, by which one believes that what Christ has promised in the sacrament will be done to him/her, that one receives grace. As Calvin noted,

"They confer or profit nothing except for those by whom they are received in faith."[3]

Given the rather generic description of a sacrament found in the *Confessio Augustana* as being any external sign or work mandated by Christ to which a divine promise has been attached, it appears that the Reformation concept could include such things as prayer, almsgiving, forgiveness of others, and so on. Thus when addressing themselves to the refutation of various Catholic sacraments, Melancthon and Calvin, in particular, adopted a more specific definition. In the *Apologia Confessionis* (1530) Melancthon defined sacraments as "ceremonies which Christ commanded to be observed and to which he added the promise of grace."[4] He specified his definition even further in the *Repetitio Confessionis Augustanae* of 1551:

> They are signs of grace, that is, ceremonies added to the promise of grace, that is of the gratuitous remission of sins and reconciliation and of the whole gift of redemption which (signs, i.e. ceremonies) have been so instituted that individuals may use them because they are a pledge and testimony which point out that the benefits promised in the Gospel pertain to individuals.[5]

This same development can be noted in the thought of Calvin. In the 1536 edition of the *Institutes*, he used the word "sacrament" to embrace all signs that God has designated to render people more certain and secure of the truth of the divine promises. In the 1539 edition of the same work, however, he defined sacraments as "ceremonies" that the Lord wishes people to perform.[6]

The core of the Reformation concept of a sacrament was that a divine promise of grace has been affixed to a visible sign, in which promise people are to place their faith. Since only Christ can make a promise of grace, the Reformers insisted that sacraments must be of divine institution. Melancthon wrote in the *Loci communes theologici* (1521) that "men can neither institute a sign of the divine will towards us nor can we adopt those signs which Scripture has employed otherwise as signifying that will."[7] Calvin likewise observed:

> A sacrament is a sign by which the testimony or promise of God is signified. Truly it cannot be signified in corporeal things and ele-

ments of this world unless they are formed and designated by the power of God for this purpose. Therefore, man cannot institute a sacrament.[8]

This conviction of the Reformers led them to accept as sacraments only those signs for which evidence of direct institution by Christ could be found. Moreover, since the Reformers looked to the Scriptures as the sole source for the Word of God that testifies to the promises of grace made by Christ, they rejected those sacraments for which no scriptural proof of immediate institution was available. In a letter to Georg Spalatin, secretary to Frederick, the elector of Saxony, Luther wrote:

> There is no reason why you or any man should expect from me any sermon on the other sacraments until I learn by what text I can prove they are sacraments. I esteem none of the others a sacrament, for that is not a sacrament save what is expressly given by a divine promise exercising our faith.[9]

It is surprising to note that even though all the Reformers spoke clearly of the need for direct evidence of institution by Christ in order for a particular sign to be considered a sacrament, they were not in agreement with one another as to which specific signs were considered to be sacraments. They all accepted that evidence can be found in the Gospels for the Lord's direct mandate for, and institution of, the sacraments of baptism and the Lord's Supper. From this point on, however, there are not only differences between the Reformers but also development within their thinking as individuals.

Luther, in the beginning of his *Babylonian Captivity*, denied that there are seven sacraments and admitted only baptism, the Lord's Supper, and penance. By the end of this treatise, however, he concluded:

> It has seemed best to restrict the name of sacrament to such promises as have signs attached to them . . . hence there are strictly speaking two sacraments in the Church of God, baptism and bread, for only in these two do we find both the divinely instituted sign and the promise of forgiveness of sins. The sacrament of penance, which I added to these two, lacks the instituted sign, and is, as I have said, nothing but a return to baptism.[10]

In the first draft of the *Loci communes theologici,* which was not published, Melancthon claimed that baptism, absolution, and the Supper are properly called sacraments.[11] But in the 1521 edition he stated that sacramental signs can be only those that have been divinely handed down as signs of grace. Moreover, since the Gospel states that only baptism and the Supper were instituted by Christ, only these two are to be considered sacraments. While he recognized the value of private confession and absolution, he held that baptism is to be considered as the sacrament of repentance.[12]

Melancthon returned to the question of whether what had been said generically about the sacraments in the *Confessio Augustana* could be applied specifically to each of the seven sacraments in Article 13 of the *Apologia Confessionis Augustanae.* Qualifying his definition of a sacrament, he appeared to assume a conciliatory stance regarding the number of the sacraments. He admitted here baptism and the Supper as sacramental ceremonies but also stated that he could agree to call penance a sacrament, for it has the mandate of Christ and a promise of grace. Furthermore, he went so far as to say that he would not be opposed to calling orders a sacrament if ordination were understood as the public approval of one's vocation to the ministry of the Word and sacraments and not to a priesthood of sacrifice. Ordination, if properly understood as such, appeared to have a mandate of God. In addition, he would grant that even though matrimony does not pertain only to the New Testament, it too has a mandate and could be considered a sacrament.[13]

Martin Bucer, like Luther, accepted only baptism and Eucharist as sacraments. Nevertheless, he made a rather startling admission concerning the ritual laying-on of hands. Calling to mind that the Apostles seemed to have used this rite for the purpose of ordination, he concluded:

> Although we have no express command of the Lord, we have nevertheless the examples of the Apostles (Acts 6:6, 13:3) and also a precept to Timothy (1 Tim 4:14; 5:22), so that it is entirely likely that the Apostles used that sign for the ordination of ministers of the Church at the command of the Lord.[14]

Although he did not call this rite a sacrament, he did observe that this ceremony has been recalled into use in the Reformed Churches.

Calvin likewise recognized only baptism and Eucharist as sacraments. With regard to the rite of imposition of hands in ordination, he claimed that he had no objection to calling it a sacrament, only that "I do not number it among the ordinary sacraments."[15] In his *De necessitate reformandae ecclesiae*, written to the Emperor Charles V justifying his rejection of five of the sacraments of the Church, he accepted marriage as an institution that God commanded to be practiced but not as a sacrament.[16]

Even though there was divergence among the Reformers as to which ceremonies were to be regarded as sacraments, none of them at any time considered extreme unction as having been instituted by Christ and thus to be accepted as a sacrament.

### The Ministers of the Sacraments

The specific rejection by the Reformers of the priest as the sole proper minister of extreme unction followed logically from their general position on the minister of the sacraments. While they unanimously spoke of the legitimate need for a recognized public ministry in the Church whose task was to proclaim the Word and administer those rites that were accepted as sacraments, they rejected any notion of this ministry as being a priesthood of sacrifice. As Calvin noted:

> Christ commanded that stewards of his Gospel and sacraments be ordained, not that sacrifices be installed. He gave a command to preach the Gospel (Mt 28:19; Mark 16:15) and feed the flock (John 21:15) not to sacrifice victims.[17]

It was Luther, however, who spoke out in the greatest detail against the priesthood of the Roman Church, not only because it appeared to have strayed from the Gospel testimony regarding the ministry, but also because it had reduced the importance and significance of the priesthood of the laity. In the *Babylonian Captivity* he writes:

> Let everyone, therefore, who knows himself to be a Christian, be assured of this, that we are all equally priests, that is to say, we have the same power in respect to the Word and the sacraments.[18]

Later on in the same chapter he qualified his assertion:

> No one may make use of this power except by the consent of the community or by the call of a superior. For what is the common property of all, no individual may arrogate to himself, unless he is called.[19]

In *An Open Letter to the Christian Nobility*, written the same year as the *Babylonian Captivity*, Luther explained his understanding of those called to minister in the Church:

> A priest in Christendom is nothing else than an office-holder . . . priests, bishops, or popes are neither different from other Christians nor superior to them except that they are charged with the administration of the Word of God and the sacraments which is their work and office.[20]

According to Luther, there is a need for a public ministry in the Church. Men are to be called to serve publicly, but only with the knowledgeable consent of the people. Their ministry is to be one of the Word rather than the priestly functions of saying mass and hearing confessions. Although he recognized that priests are to be publicly called, Luther did not accept that one becomes a priest through ordination, for he looked upon all Christians as priests.

As a result, when speaking of the various functions traditionally attributed to priests, Luther held that they are common to all Christians. In his *Concerning the Ministry*, he recalled Christ's command "Do this in remembrance of me" (Luke 22:19) and related it to the ministry of the Word that pertains to all followers of Christ:

> All of them are given the right and command to hold the Lord in remembrance, so that God may be praised and glorified in his marvelous deeds. He means that we should remember him not by offering masses in hidden corners or by enforced meditations, but by a public ministry of the Word for the salvation of those who hear.[21]

Reflecting on these same words of the Lord with regard to the function of consecrating or administering the Eucharist, Luther wrote:

> We hold that this function, too, like the priesthood, belongs to all, and this we assert, not on our own authority, but that of Christ who at the Last Supper said, "Do this in remembrance of me.". . . Christ spoke this word to all those then present and to those who in the future would be at the table to eat this bread and drink this cup. So it follows that what is given here is given to all.[22]

For Luther, the function of binding and loosing from sin, especially when understood in the context of the words of Matthew 18:15, in a similar fashion belongs to the whole Church and to each of its members, "both as regards its authority and its various uses."[23] He interpreted "to bind and to loose" in this case as meaning the proclamation and application of the Gospel message of God's forgiveness. Finally, refuting what he perceived to be a perverted understanding of the Eucharist in the Roman Church, he concluded, "Today no other sacrifice is possible than that which is sacrificed and perfected by the Word of God; and since the Word is common to all, the sacrifice too must be one pertaining to all."[24]

Luther summarized all of his conclusions by noting that since these mandates are the common rights of all Christians,

> no one individual can arise by his own authority and arrogate to himself alone what belongs to all . . . the community rights demand that one, or as many as the community chooses, shall be chosen or approved who, in the name of all with these rights, shall perform these functions publicly.[25]

Thus Luther seemed to imply a distinction on the basis of which he could say that while all Christians are priests, not all are ministers.

It is evident, therefore, that the Reformers did not deny the importance of a public ministry. They were rejecting the error they perceived in the Roman Church's transforming this ministry into a sacrificial priesthood. Furthermore, they reacted against the Church's notion of ordination, according to which it was accepted as a sacrament wherein those powers and mandates that the Lutherans saw as having been entrusted by Christ to the whole Church were conferred upon certain individuals. They recognized that a public ministry was necessary principally in the interests of good order in the Church.

When the Reformers claimed that all Christians have the "power" to administer the sacraments because all members of the Church are to be considered priests, they did not specify exactly what they meant by this "power." It appears that they understood it to be that power without which there could not be a valid proclamation of the Word or administration of the sacraments, even though it could only be exercised when a person was correctly called forth by the community or, in the case of an emergency and in the absence of an acknowledged public minister, on one's own initiative.[26]

## The Teaching of the Continental Reformers on Extreme Unction and Its Minister

Luther, Melancthon, and Calvin were the only Continental Reformers who in any systematic way addressed themselves to the sacrament of extreme unction. In each case their primary concern seemed to be the refusal to accept it as a sacrament. Their reasoning followed two paths: first, since no evidence could be found for the direct institution of this anointing by Christ, they concluded that this ritual could only be of human invention. Second, granting the ritual described by James, they attempted to illustrate from the contemporary practice of the Church that it had failed to remain faithful to the words of James 5:14-15, the very words that the Church accepted as the authority for the promulgation of this sacrament. It is within this context of accusing the Church of having erred in its practice that the Reformers treated the specific question concerning the minister of extreme unction.

### *Martin Luther*

Luther began by doubting that the Epistle of James was even written by the Apostle James or that it could in any way be considered apostolic.[27] He then proceeded to the principal point of his argument:

> Even if the Apostle James did write it, I should say that no Apostle has the right on his own authority to institute a sacrament, that is, to give a divine promise with a sign attached; for this belongs to Christ alone . . . and we read nowhere in the Gospel of this sacrament of extreme unction.[28]

Moreover, Luther strongly criticized the Church for its practice of administering this anointing only to the dying:

> For he [James] did not desire it to be an extreme unction or to be administered only to the dying; but he says quite generally: "If any man be sick," not "If any man be dying."[29]

Noting that the Epistle instructs that a sick person be anointed and prayers offered that he or she be healed and raised up, so that in fact this anointing will not be an extreme unction, Luther used a play on words to attack the Church's administration of this sacrament *in extremis:* "They affirm what the scriptures deny, and deny what they affirm."[30] He went on to say that if the Romans believed that sacraments are always effective signs of what they signify, then this anointing should be an effective sign of health and recovery. By overlooking this effect of healing and administering the sacrament only to those near death, he concluded that either James lied in making this a sacrament or this rite of anointing is no sacrament. "If it is extreme unction, it does not heal, but gives way to the disease; but if it heals, it cannot be extreme unction."[31] Although the Church professed that both the forgiveness of sins and the healing of the infirm, if it would be to the person's spiritual benefit, were effects of this sacrament, the actual practice of the Church could only lead Luther to conclude that bodily cure had become an almost non-existent effect despite the words of James.

There seemed to be a sense, however, in which Luther saw a value to a ritual anointing of the sick. In his writings on the Last Supper (1528), he noted:

> I would allow this anointing with oil if it were observed according to the custom of the Gospel and the opinion of James 5, but that a sacrament results from this, I pass. For just as it is more convenient to preach to the living among the tombs of the dead about death and eternal life than to offer vigils and masses for the deceased, so too it would be very opportune to approach a sick person, pray for him, exhort him to do good, and if they wish or he himself desires, anoint him with oil in the name of the Lord; in all cases this anointing is not to be considered a sacrament.[32]

Therefore, according to Luther, if any ritual anointing was to be effective, it would be because of the prayer of faith. Reading James 5 as saying "the prayer offered in faith will save the sick man, the Lord will raise him up and if he be in sins they will be forgiven him," Luther observed that this prayer is to be understood in the light of James 1:6, "But let him ask in faith without a doubt in his mind," and the words of Christ, "Whatsoever you ask, believe that you shall receive; and it shall be done unto you."[33] It was in this sense that Luther was able to conclude:

> I do not deny that forgiveness of sins and peace are granted through extreme unction; not because it is a sacrament divinely instituted but because he who receives it believes that these blessings are granted to him.[34]

Finally, commenting on James' instruction that "the presbyters of the Church are to be brought in," Luther wrote:

> I have my doubts, however, whether he would have us understand priests when he says presbyters, that is elders. For one who is an elder is not therefore a priest or minister, so that the suspicion is justified that the Apostle desired the older and more serious men in the Church to visit the sick; these should perform a work of mercy and pray in faith and thus heal the sick person.[35]

## Melancthon

In the *Loci communes theologici* of 1521, Melancthon referred to Luther's treatment of extreme unction in the *Babylonian Captivity* and concluded that "extreme unction is more an ancient rite than a sign of grace."[36] Melancthon regarded this ritual, like confirmation, as simply an ecclesiastical rite which, because it does not have an express mandate of Christ, is not to be accepted as necessary for salvation.[37] In the second edition of the *Apologia* (1531) he concluded, "For that reason, it is not useless to distinguish these rites [confirmation and extreme unction] from the above rites [baptism, the Lord's Supper, and absolution], which have the express mandate of God and a clear promise of grace."[38]

Melancthon explained how the anointing referred to by James was to be understood. Calling to mind the fact that God gave to the patriarchs and the prophets the gift of healing as signs substantiating their authority, Melancthon asserted that Christ, in the new covenant, brought back this old custom and himself taught by the gift of healing. When he sent the Apostles out on their mission, he instructed them also to cure the sick. This gift of healing remained in the Church even after the Apostles, and Melancthon noted that even now many are healed by the prayers of the Church. With regard to the Roman rite of extreme unction, however, he wrote:

The rite of anointing which we now have is only a superstitious ceremony; it has come to resemble an invocation of the dead, which is impious. Thus this anointing with its additions is to be rejected.[39]

It is within the context of these "additions" that he criticized the practice of the Church, especially that of administering extreme unction *in extremis*. According to Melancthon, this anointing was originally intended to be a medical cure and given as a gift of healing. The present practice of the Church was for him further proof that extreme unction was to be regarded as nothing more than a superstitious ceremony. Moreover, he looked upon the formularies used for consecrating the oil as magical incantations, and he argued that any anointings for which this oil was used were not to be tolerated.[40] Melancthon did not, however, make any specific mention of the restriction that only priests could administer extreme unction as being one of the ways in which, according to him, the Church had erred in deviating from the rite of anointing as found in James.

*Calvin*

Like Luther and Melancthon, Calvin could not find any evidence in the Scriptures for either a direct mandate of God or a promise of grace for extreme unction, and he concluded that it is not a sacrament and can be no more than a ceremony of human origin. Furthermore, Calvin regarded the Church's use of anointing as histrionic hypocrisy, much like the use of the imposition of hands in the sacrament of confirmation. He noted that even though we read in Mark that the Apostles used an anointing with oil to cure the sick on their first mission, the cure was not attributed to the anointing. The Apostles employed this anointing simply as a sign to instruct the common people that the power of cures was due to the action of the Spirit and not to be mistakenly attributed to themselves. As a result, Calvin refused to attribute any higher or mystical significance to this unction with oil.[41]

Calvin explained the parallel between anointing and the imposition of hands by referring to the time when Peter and John imposed hands on the Samaritans, who, though they had been baptized in the name of Christ, had not yet received the Spirit. After praying over them, those upon whom they imposed hands received the Spirit. In other words, according to Calvin, Christ intended that the visible and manifest graces of the Spirit be administered through the imposition of hands, which ritual was simply a gesture whereby the Apostles signified that they were commending to God those whom they so identified.

Calvin went on to explain that the purpose of James' description of the anointing of the sick was to draw attention to that time in the Church when the initial preaching of the Gospel was accompanied by miraculous powers, cures, and manifest operations, all of which served to render the Gospel an object of admiration. Just as Christ and the Apostles frequently used ordinary things, not as instruments of grace or cures, but as signs of these miraculous deeds, an anointing with oil was used as a sign of the gift of healing received from the Spirit.

Although Calvin admitted that the Spirit is just as present to people today and is as ready to heal the infirm, God no longer displays those visible powers or dispenses miracles as he did at the hands of the Apostles. Thus, if the gift of cures which pertained to that unique era in the Church had now passed, so too those ritual gestures that signified the miraculous healings should be discontinued or used only by someone endowed with the special power of healing.[42]

Accepting the fact that the Church professed to follow the instruction given by James even after the early period of the Church, Calvin likewise criticized the Roman practice of administering this anointing to "half-dead cadavers." He noted that James speaks only of an anointing with ordinary oil, and that Mark 6:13 makes no reference to the Apostles using any consecrated oil. Thus he asked on what basis the Church insisted that the matter of this ritual had to be oil consecrated by a bishop. Moreover, he accused the Church, in claiming that sins are remitted by this ritual anointing, of having abused the authority of James, who, according to Calvin, was simply saying that the prayers of the faithful by which the afflicted person is commended to God would not be futile. Finally, in the *Institutes* of 1536, he wrote, "James wishes that the sick be anointed by the elders of the Church, but these [Romans] allow only a sacrificing priest as anointer."[43] He seemed to detect a contradiction on the part of the Church in making this restriction, for in the same paragraph he referred to Pope Innocent I as an authority legitimating the practice that not only presbyters but all Christians were to use this oil for anointing when they or their dependents needed it.

## The Reformation Writings in England

The reform movement in England took place later than on the Continent, and its writings were frequently the results of an amalgamation of Lutheran thought and traditional Roman theology. Although the Council of Trent responded chiefly to the Continental Reformers, the Reformation writings in England prior to Trent, especially those on the question of the institution and the numbering of the sacraments, further elucidate the thrust of Reformation sacramental theology that led to the rejection of extreme unction.

There are four principal documents from the period between 1536 and 1543 that might be termed "confessions of faith." The "Ten Articles of 1536," which arose out of a convocation between the school of New Learning, which championed the teachings of the Continental Reformers, and the school of Old Learning, which reacted to the new theology of the Reformation, contain only a sketchy presentation of the sacraments. Reference is made to three sacraments, namely, baptism, Eucharist, and penance; the remaining four sacraments are neither affirmed nor denied.[44]

The following year there was published the *Bishops' Book*, which was the result of a compromise between the pro- and anti-Reformation factions of the English episcopate.[45] In this document all seven of the Roman sacraments are treated and referred to as being worthy of the name "sacrament." The *Bishops' Book* notes a difference in dignity and necessity between baptism, Eucharist, and penance and the other four. The source of this distinction rests upon the opinion that only the three were instituted by Christ as certain instruments necessary for salvation. As for the others, they are "holy godly signs whereby and by the prayer of the minister, there be given and conferred some certain and special gifts of the Holy Ghost necessary for Christian men to have for one godly purpose or other."[46] The *Bishops' Book* accepted a variety of modes of sacramental institution for these four sacraments. With regard to extreme unction, it notes that it is on the authority of James that the use of this rite is recommended. Like confirmation, extreme unction arose out of a decision by the Fathers of the Church, who determined that it was "convenient" to observe this recommendation of James.[47]

The "Thirteen Articles of 1538" were drafted at a meeting of a number of Lutherans and English churchmen headed by Thomas Cranmer, who was considered to be the leader of the school of New Learning. Since the conference broke down and for a period of time Cranmer's influence dwindled, these articles were never published. They are important, however, not only because they are considered to be somewhat of a basis for later confessions of faith but also because they demonstrate the strong influence of the Continental Reformation thinking on the English scene.

The definition of a sacrament found in these articles is greatly reminiscent of that found in article 13 of the *Confessio Augustana:*

> We teach that sacraments which were instituted through the word of God not only are marks of profession among Christians, but more important are certain specific testimonies and efficacious signs of grace and the good will of God toward us through which God invisibly operates in us and diffuses his grace in us invisibly if in fact we receive them correctly so that through them, faith is stirred up and confirmed in those who use them.[48]

*Chapter Seven*

# THE RESPONSE OF THE PRE-TRIDENTINE CATHOLIC APOLOGISTS

Prior to the Council of Trent, a number of Catholic theologians had begun to respond to the attacks of the Continental Reformers. An examination of the writings of several of these Catholic scholars provides an insight into the theological mentality of the Church prior to and at the time of the convocation of Trent.

## The Sacraments in General

When treating of the sacraments in general, these writers directed their arguments primarily against what they called the Reformation *"ratio sacramenti."* The Reformers defined a sacrament as an external sign or, more specifically, a ceremony to which Christ had affixed a promise of grace for which direct evidence could be found in the Scriptures. In the case of several of the sacraments, including extreme unction, where this scriptural evidence for any direct institution by Christ was lacking, they refused to accept them as sacraments.

The Catholic theologians of this period adopted the Scholastic definition of a sacrament as an *"invisibilis gratiae visibile signum efficax"* ("a visible, efficacious sign of invisible grace").[1] According to the theology of the Church, a sacrament consisted in a visible element or sign and the word or prayer, and these two factors sufficed for a complete *"ratio sacramenti."*[2] As a result, the Catholic theologians took exception to the Reformers' claim that there had to be that divine promise which effectively promised and exhibited the grace of God to the recipient of the sacrament. According to the apologists, even though a word, prayer, or formula is an essential constituent of the sacrament, this word is not always promissory. As the theologian Cochlaeus wrote, sacraments can "legitimately be accomplished and give grace without these formulas of divine promise which you [Luther] prescribe for us as a new Messiah or master of ceremonies."[3]

In order to disprove the Protestants' claim, the Catholic authors demonstrated their position by noting that in baptism, Eucharist, and penance, which Luther accepted as sacraments, the formulas used are not promissory. They noted that in baptism, instead of the Marcan phrase that Luther frequently cited, "He who believes and is baptized will be saved," the words of Matthew's Gospel, "I baptize you in the name of . . . ," are used as the formula. This is not because Christ, the evangelists, or the Church has overlooked or disregarded the promise of grace made by Christ, but simply that the promissory formula is not necessary for the substance of the sacrament of baptism.

With regard to the Eucharist, John Fisher wrote:

> The Eucharist has no obvious promise of grace especially if one denies that the sixth chapter of John refers to the Eucharist, just as Luther altogether contends. For the promise regarding the remission of sins which is therein commemorated is without a doubt because of the shedding of blood on the cross and not because of his drinking from the chalice.[4]

Concerning penance, the observation was made that instead of the words "Whatever you shall loose on earth shall be loosed in heaven . . . ," the Church has always used the form "I absolve you from your sins . . . ."

In light of the sacramental forms which the Church had employed in the past and which were presently being used, Cochlaeus concluded:

> Are we to abandon the ancient form of baptizing which Christ instituted and the Church, up to this day, has held so that we may receive a new formula of baptism from you? . . . Neither in penance nor in the Eucharist do we use your formulas, but those (which) antiquity has passed on and which today all the Church observes.[5]

Having rejected the claim that the promissory formulas pertain to the substance of a sacrament, the Catholic theologians also addressed the Reformation concept of sacramental institution. The Reformers insisted that only Christ could make that promise of divine grace which, according to their definition, was an essential constitutive element of a sacrament, and so they accepted only those signs or ceremonies as sacraments for which there is evidence from the Scriptures of direct institution by Christ.

In response, the apologists emphasized the role of tradition in the Church. They noted that much of what Christ and his disciples preached and taught is not recorded in the Scriptures. Many things in the Church that are to be kept and observed have been demonstrated by the Holy Spirit and passed on by tradition. As Eck remarked:

> The Church observes many things in her rites and ceremonies on the basis of the Holy Spirit and the tradition of the Apostles and the holy fathers which, even if they are not expressly found in the sacred writings, are by no means in opposition to them or disagree with them.[6]

In an effort to defend the role of tradition, the *Assertio septem sacramentorum*, attributed to Henry VIII, demonstrated a way in which Luther could be said to believe in what is tantamount to the infallibility of the Church: "His [Luther's] own words are these, 'Truly the Church has this faculty that it can discern the Word of God from the word of men.'"[7] Thus if Luther admits that the Church has this power, he must admit that this power can come only from God. By this same power, the *Assertio* continued, the Church can also discern between the divine and human sense of Scripture; otherwise the Church would be liable to fall into error. Furthermore, since God instructs the Church even in things that are not written, "it appears, therefore, by Luther's confessing the Church to have a faculty of discerning the words of God from the words of men, it has no less power to discern between divine institution and the traditions of men."[8] The author of the *Assertio* also reminded Luther that it is out of this same living tradition of the Church that the canon of Scripture arose: "You ought to believe concerning things which are not in the Gospels when (as St. Augustine says) 'You could never know which is the Scripture itself, but by the tradition of the Church.' "[9]

The general argument of the theology of that time regarding the force of tradition rested on the fact that since the Church has received power directly from Christ and is instructed by the Holy Spirit, both of whom are equal in their divinity, power, and teaching, then

> whatever the Holy Spirit, after Christ, through the Apostles or through the other doctors and rectors in the Church has spiritually undertaken or will yet undertake is to have no less force than that which Christ himself from the beginning as man did and instituted. Therefore, that which is ecclesiastically instituted is a divine, not a human, work.[10]

Based on this understanding of the role of tradition, the Catholic response to the Reformers, as noted in the *Assertio*, was to ask if the Church could so rashly have instituted a sacrament and for so many years placed her hope in nothing more than an empty sign.

When discussing the role played by Christ in the institution of those sacraments for which there is no scriptural evidence of direct divine institution, these apologists employed a variety of expressions, some of which sound similar to those used by the Scholastic theologians of the Middle Ages. They spoke of the institution of these sacraments as being attributed to the Lord, not by his exhibiting the sacrament but on "the example of the Lord,"[11] or *"by promising,"*[12] or "by his confirming what had been instituted by God before the incarnation,"[13] or "begun by Christ,"[14] and so on. It was then left to the Apostles and the early Fathers to "pass on," "promulgate," even to determine the specific form some of these sacraments would take.

In defending the position of the Church regarding sacramental institution, the sixteenth-century Catholic apologists placed great emphasis on the authority of the Apostles, the early Fathers, and the Church, not only to prove the existence of those sacraments rejected by the Reformers because of the lack of any direct scriptural evidence of their institution by Christ, but also to explain and to justify the particular form and mode of celebration that these sacraments may have assumed down through the centuries. It is important to note that such a notion of sacramental institution was prevalent in the Church at the time when the Council of Trent began to formulate its response to the writings of the Reformers.

## The Catholic Apologists on Extreme Unction and Its Minister

When the Catholic apologists dealt with extreme unction, they were primarily concerned with responding to the Reformers' denial of its sacramentality and divine institution. As a result, most of those theologians do not include a systematic treatment of all the aspects of this sacrament in their writings. In general, they all said that extreme unction is a sacrament and was instituted by Christ. Pirstinger and Herborn looked especially to the command given by Christ to the Apostles in Mark 6:13 as evidence of this.

With regard to the role played by James, Pirstinger taught that the Holy Spirit, through James, commanded the sick to be anointed in the name of the Lord.[15] Quoting Romans 15, where Paul claims that he has done nothing other than that which was done by Christ, Herborn said that James is simply testifying to the observance of this rite by the primitive Church, which was done according to the example and precept of Christ.[16] According to Eck, James promulgated this sacrament instituted by Christ. The author of the *Assertio*, refusing to discuss whether or not an Apostle has the power of instituting a sacrament, said that James delivered to the people that which he had received from Christ.[17]

Cajetan appears to be the sole exception among the Catholic writers of this period concerning the traditional interpretation of the texts of Mark and James. In discussing the apostolic anointing of the sick attested to in Mark 6:13, he wrote:

> It is true, this anointing is not understood to be sacramental as is extreme unction which the Church uses, but a certain beginning. It appears that they [the Twelve] used oil to cure, not for administering a sacrament. It also appears that health followed immediately; otherwise the power of the healing oil would not have been known.[18]

Cajetan departed even more radically from the common tradition in commenting on James 5:14-15:

Neither from the words nor from the effect do these words speak of the sacramental anointing of extreme unction, but more of the anointing which the Lord Jesus instituted in the Gospel to be exercised by the disciples on the sick. For the text does not say: "Let him who is sick unto death," but says absolutely, "Let anyone who is sick"; and it says the effect is the alleviation of the sick and only speaks of the remission of sins conditionally, whereas extreme unction is only properly given at the time of death and directly (as the form says) tends to the remission of sins. Beyond this is the fact that James prescribes that many presbyters be called in to the sick person both to pray and to anoint, which is foreign to the rite of extreme unction.[19]

Even though the Reformers included with their rejection of the sacramentality of extreme unction a criticism of the way the Church had deviated from James in its practice of anointing the sick, these pre-Tridentine theologians did not offer a thorough defense of what was the current discipline of the Church regarding this sacrament. In fact, the *Assertio septem sacramentorum* referred to the criticisms that Luther made in an almost derisive manner. "For what else he says are but Trifles, whereby he takes occasion to laugh as if the Church did not do well in observing this sacrament."[20] As a result, they did not bother to justify matters such as the valid matter of the sacrament being oil consecrated by a bishop or the specific form used by the Church in administering the anointing, even though both of these factors are clearly a development from the words of James, as the Reformers had noted.

Several of the Catholic authors did discuss the validity of administering this sacrament to the dying. The *Assertio* observed that the words of James do not indicate any light sickness but refer to a grave illness, as demonstrated by the prayers of the ritual. Moreover, since it is the spirit and not the body that is to live forever, the author of the *Assertio* concluded that quite obviously spiritual effects are to be understood.[21] Pirstinger called attention to the spiritual weakness and guilt left by mortal sin as well as venial sins, which weaken the human spirit. According to him, these are removed by extreme unction. Furthermore, given the very necessity of dying, a sacrament is required at the time of death as a unique remedy for reconciling human beings with God. Through extreme unction, they are cured of spiritual infirmity, so there is no contradiction in administering this sacrament *in extremis*.[22] Eck, moreover, referred to the *De visitatione infirmorum*, which has traditionally but inaccurately been attributed to Augustine, as instructing that "the sick person should confess, communicate, and receive the anointing."[23] Apparently Eck considered that the proper place for extreme unction was as the last of the three sacraments to be given to the dying.

Two other apologists, Ruard Tapper and Peter DeSoto, wrote shortly after Trent's promulgation of its teaching on extreme unction. Their writings serve to further illustrate several opinions present at the time of the Council. Tapper was of the Thomistic opinion that extreme unction liberated the soul principally from the remnants of sin as a preparation for glory and insisted that this anointing should be given only to the dying. Extreme unction was to be accompanied by confession and Eucharist, both of which, according to Tapper, were to precede the administration of the anointing.[24]

DeSoto, arguing from the text of James, was insistent on tradition's recognition of the possibility of a physical cure as one of the effects of extreme unction. He wrote:

> The words "the prayer of faith will save the sick person" are referred also to the other effect which doctors truly associate with this sacrament, that is, that it brings health to the body. For since it is more convenient for the salvation of the sick person or the Church, they are not to doubt that it can happen that one be cured by this sacrament: certainly not miraculously and suddenly, for now is not the time of miracles, but by the providence of God and virtue of the sacrament and also other means which many experts admit to themselves.[25]

Therefore, when the sixteenth-century apologists, with the possible exception of DeSoto, did respond to the Reformers' criticism of administering this sacrament to those *in extremis*, their justification of this practice followed from an undocumented assumption that the primary effect of extreme unction had always been the spiritual effect, that is, the remission of sins and the curing of spiritual weaknesses. Their apparent complete acceptance of this restriction of the sacrament would seem to indicate an acknowledgment on their part that the Church had the competence to make the other changes regarding extreme unction that the Reformers were rejecting.

Concerning the question of the minister of the anointing, the majority of these theologians said nothing more than the simple statement of fact that the proper minister of extreme unction is the priest. Tapper, however, specifically referred to canon 4 of Trent regarding the minister of extreme unction and interpreted the "presbyters" of the James text as priests. In so doing, he made an interesting observation concerning the disputed text from the letter of Pope Innocent I:

> Although in the Scriptures, sometimes it [presbyter] is the name of the episcopal function: in B. Peter (1 Peter 5:1), the word here is general, including simply priests as well: just as Innocent I, who was asked about this same thing, teaches: "On the other hand," he says, "it seems to us superfluous to add that it be ambiguous regarding the bishop of what there is no doubt is permitted to priests. For it is said regarding priests because bishops, hampered by occupations, cannot go to the suffering." Innocent does not teach in this place that it is permitted to laity to administer this sacrament when he says that it is permitted not only to priests but also to all Christians to use this sacrament for anointing in their own necessity and that of their family. For the word *inungendo* has a passive meaning, not an active one, which fact is manifest from the particular preceding point that there is no doubt that this opinion of James ought to be understood of the faithful sick.[26]

This statement of Tapper on the proper minister of extreme unction is significant not only because it indicates that the papal text was known at the time of Trent but also because, as Calvin noted, it illustrates that this document was associated with a theory that, at least at one time, this sacrament was administered by the laity. It is also interesting to note the similarity between Tapper's grammatical interpretation of the papal letter and that of one of the more contemporary schools of opinion which refutes the position that this document and other similar texts are evidence that there was a period in the Church when the lay administering of this sacramental anointing was a common and legitimate practice.

*Chapter Eight*

# THE RESPONSE OF THE COUNCIL OF TRENT

In responding to the Reformers' teaching on the sacraments, the Council of Trent adopted a twofold method: it addressed itself to various questions concerning the sacraments in general, and then it treated each of the sacraments individually. The basic procedure employed by the Council was as follows. A list was submitted to the Council containing the errors of the heretics. The theologians were asked to examine each of these articles in order to determine which of them were to be considered "either heretical or erroneous and for that reason to be condemned by the Council."[1] As a result of their investigation, the theologians were instructed to classify the articles according to those that had already been condemned and should be condemned again, and those that should not be condemned, with the reasons for this decision. Then they were to add any error that they also found to be worthy of censure and not previously included in the listing. The list of articles was then turned over to the bishops for their deliberation and eventual promulgation.

## The Reply of Trent on the Sacraments in General

One of the principal claims Trent had to deal with was the Protestant accusation that the Church had accepted as sacraments certain ceremonies that lacked explicit evidence of sacramental institution by Christ and therefore could be considered nothing more than vain, empty human inventions. Thus the Council was faced with the task of affirming both the number and the divine origin of the Church's sacraments. Moreover, since the Reformers pointed to what they called the false sacraments as examples of how the Church had abused its authority, Trent attempted to designate exactly what the authority of the Church was with regard to sacramental matters.

*Sacramental institution*

While the Protestant rejection of the septenary numbering of the sacraments was among the list of errors submitted to the theologians, there was not included on this list any article regarding sacramental institution or the need for evidence from the Scriptures of this fact. The theologians affirmed that there are seven signs, no more, no less, that could be properly called sacraments, and any claim to the contrary was against the universal consent of the Church and had already been condemned in previous councils.[2] Implied in this affirmation was the fact of the divine origin of these sacraments. It was during the discussion that the whole question of sacramental institution and the need for scriptural evidence was introduced by the theologians themselves.[3] On January 29, 1547, the original list of articles containing the errors of the Reformers, together with new articles added at the recommendation of the theologians, was submitted to the Council Fathers.

Nearly all the bishops agreed that the denial of the septenary numbering should be condemned principally on the basis of the teaching of the Council of Florence. Moreover, since no one except Christ can institute a sacrament, the bishops approved the article introduced by the theologians on sacramental institution. However, the consensus of the bishops regarding the article concerning evidence in the Scriptures for each of the sacraments was that because all the sacraments are found in the Scriptures either "implicitly or explicitly," the article as submitted by the theologians should not be condemned.

Among the canons on the sacraments in general promulgated by the Council on March 3, 1547, the first states:

> If anyone should say that the sacraments of the New Law were not all instituted by our Lord Jesus Christ or are more or less than seven,

that is baptism, confirmation, . . . or even that any one of these seven is not truly and properly a sacrament, A.S. (DS 1601).

Consequently, Trent substantiated the fact that each of the seven sacraments of the Church is truly and properly a sacrament by recalling the authoritative teaching of the Church and by stating the divine origin of the sacraments simply by proclaiming the fact of their institution by Christ. The Council Fathers did not, however, indicate how Christ instituted them.

Neither in this canon nor in any other canon on the sacraments in general is there a reference to the article "It is not a sacrament unless it is found in the Scriptures." According to the *Acta*, this was omitted because "it seemed unnecessary to express this, since it is said in canon 1 that all the sacraments were instituted by Christ" (CT 5, p. 986). It may have been that the Fathers felt it was unnecessary to address the Reformers' insistence on scriptural evidence for the institution of the sacraments because the very statement of institution implies the presence of some reference in the Scriptures for each sacrament, even though this reference might not in each case explicate the exact relationship between Christ and the particular sacrament. Or it might be that, according to the mind of the Council, it is not necessary in the case of each and every sacrament that there be a reference in the Scriptures in order that it be taught that Christ instituted all the sacraments. Regardless of which hypothesis is correct, what is clear is the fact that even though some of the theologians and bishops at the Council were aware of the theological debate on the mode of sacramental institution by Christ, as evidenced by the interventions in the *Acta*, by remaining silent regarding the manner in which Christ instituted the sacraments the Council was purposely avoiding promulgating in this matter what was controverted within the Church.[4]

*Trent and the authority of the Church over the sacraments*

The question of the Church's authority over the sacraments was first addressed when the Council, in Session 7, discussed the Reformers' claim that any pastor has the power to prolong, abbreviate, and change at will the forms of the sacraments (CT 5, p. 836). In addition to questioning where the authority lies for changing the form of the sacraments, this article also appeared to be a denial of the power of the Church to impose upon its ministers a ritual for the administration of the sacraments.

When speaking of changes in the "form of the sacrament," most of the theologians seemed to be referring to changes in the ritual ceremonies, and it is at this point that there first arose in the Council the distinction that additions or subtractions are possible "as long as the substance is kept" (CT 5, p. 846). Exactly what was meant by this condition, however, was not delineated by the Council. Several of the theologians were of the opinion that the authority of the Church to make changes extended beyond the ceremonies within which the sacraments are administered to the matter and form of the sacraments, at least where it is evident that there has been a development from the testimony of the Scriptures.[5] In the canon finally approved by the Council, the authority of the Church to determine and approve and mandate the rites to be used in their administration was clearly affirmed (DS 1613).

This issue of the Church's authority over the sacraments arose again when Trent responded to the Reformers' teaching on the Eucharist, in particular their refusal to accept the Church's right to restrict the laity and non-celebrating priests to communicating under only one species. Among the errors of the heretics on the Eucharist presented to the Council on February 3, 1547, there was included:

> It is of divine law that even the people communicate under both species, and therefore they sin who force the people to use one species. And even though the Council [of Constance] prescribed that the people may communicate under both species, it is in any case to be communicated under one (CT 5, p. 859).

The *Acta* note that this error was taken from the *Confessio Augustana*, which held that communicating under both kinds has the direct mandate of the Lord, " 'All of you must drink from it,' he said" (Matt 26:27; CT 5, p. 870).

The onus of the Council's deliberations was to demonstrate from the Scriptures, apostolic tradition, and the custom of the Church that since Communion under both kinds for the people was not of divine law, the Church is perfectly free to make this change. In other words, if communication under both species were of divine law, the Church could not have prohibited it for the laity, which in fact it had done at the Council of Constance. Any position that challenged this fact would be not only a pertinacious denial of the rightful authority of the Church but also an accusation that the Church had erred. Such a position would be worthy of condemnation. As a result, a number of the Fathers offered different interpretations of Matthew 26:27, most of which attempted to justify the practice of the laity communicating only under one kind.

The discussion on this article was discontinued and was not resumed until the Council returned from Bologna to Trent in September 1551. At that time the majority of the Council Fathers were of the opinion that the teaching of the Reformers should be condemned again because of its implication that the Church had erred in restricting the laity to communicating only under one species. At the same time, however, there were several bishops who, while accepting the practice of the Church, held the opinion that because of the general nature of Christ's words, the position that it is not of divine law that all persons be communicated under both kinds could not be defended.[6] Ottavio Preconio, bishop of Monopoli, made the following interesting observation:

> Truly, because the Church has determined it to be done otherwise, it is to be maintained just as the Church itself has changed many other things concerning divine life, such as the form of baptism, the renouncing of walking stick and traveling bag (Matt 10:9), circumcision, *"de sanguine et suffocato,"* and similar other matters that the Church was able to change. This article, therefore, is heretical not because it is against the divine law, but because it is against the Church (CT 7, p. 158).

These rather strong interventions prompted one of the Council presidents, Sebastiano Pighino, the archbishop of Manfredonia, to make a distinction between an "institution" of divine law and a "precept" of divine law. Thereupon he commented, "An institution does not oblige all, just as orders and matrimony; a precept however obliges. But this practice [Communion under both kinds] is not a precept but an institution" (CT 7, p. 178). He supported his contention by demonstrating that the various references from the Scriptures were not preceptive, and concluded that the Church cannot change the essentials of divine law.

On October 3, 1551, the following canon was presented to the Fathers:

> If anyone should say that it is necessary for salvation and prescribed by divine law that each and every Christian communicate under both kinds or that the Church had sinned thus far in that it communicated laity and non-celebrating priests under only the one species of bread, A.S. (CT 7, p. 174).

Three days later the Council was notified that the Protestants had petitioned to come and be heard by the Fathers. They had also requested that the Council refrain from treating and publishing several articles until their arrival, one of which concerned Communion under both kinds. The bishops agreed, and discussion on this article was deferred until the period following Session 20.

Even though the predominant reason given by most of the bishops for condemning the position of the Reformers regarding Communion under both kinds was that it challenged the authority of the Church, there were those who on the basis of Scripture felt that communicating both the Body and Blood of the Lord was not only a divine law but also a precept of Christ to be followed by all. Nevertheless, these same bishops continued to support the competency of the Church to make a change in this practice, and it can only be concluded that they viewed the authority of the Church to be such that it extended even to matters directly prescribed by divine law.[7]

Given that the Council left unresolved how it understood the relationship between the Church's authority over the sacraments and what is considered to be of divine law, the deliberations regarding Communion under both kinds offer no further insight for interpreting the exact meaning of Trent's basic position that the Church has the competence to make any changes in sacramental matters, as long as those modifications do not affect the "substance of the sacraments." Since the Council had earlier refrained from determining the manner in which Christ instituted the sacraments, it is not surprising that it did not specify what was meant by *substantia sacramentorum*, other than that it was that over which the Church has no power to initiate change. It is only by examining the Council's teaching on the individual sacraments that it can be determined whether or not these limits of the authority of the Church have been more specifically identified.

*Trent and the general question of the ministers of the sacarments*

Canon 10 on the sacraments in general promulgated at Session 7 states: "If anyone should say that all Christians have power for administering the Word and all the sacraments, A.S." (DS 1610). This canon was the fruit of the discussion over the article submitted to the Council that "all Christians of either sex have equal power in administering the Word and sacraments" (CT 5, p. 836). The *Acta* cite Luther's *Babylonian Captivity* as the source from which this error was taken. While Luther did speak out against the emphasis placed by the Church on its official ministry as a sacrificial priesthood to the detriment of the priesthood of all believers, it was only in a qualified way that he could maintain that all people could administer the Word and sacraments.

The opinions of the theologians regarding this article were not unanimous. The key phrase in the debate seemed to be "equal power." Several of them gave the article only the theological note of "false,"[8] and the Servite theologian Lorenzo Mazochi suggested that the words "except in case of necessity" be added.[9] The consensus, however, was that this article should be classified among those that had already been condemned by previous councils and that it should be so again without any declaration.[10] They cited the Fourth Council of Carthage and the Councils of Constance and Florence as their authority.

At the Fourth Council of Carthage, the question was whether or not lay persons, especially women, are permitted to teach, and in the case of canon 100, whether women may baptize.[11] The Council of Constance addressed the denial of the Church's authority to limit people from preaching the Word.[12] The *Decretum pro Arme-*

*nis* of the Council of Florence treated the minister of the sacraments individually. In so doing, the Council of Florence noted that even though the regular minister of baptism is the priest, in the case of necessity lay people, even pagans, can baptize, as long as they intend to do what the Church does. It stated that the bishop is the minister of confirmation, recognizing that in certain circumstances and with the appropriate dispensation a priest can administer this sacrament. The *Decretum* simply notes that the priest is the minister of extreme unction and, when he has the required commission of a superior, also of penance. There is no explicit statement regarding the minister of Eucharist or matrimony. It appears as though these councils were principally concerned with the good order of the Church. If so, the "power of the minister" referred to by them would be more one of "authorization," that is, the power of those who in fact have been designated to teach or to administer the sacraments.

The bishops were also in agreement that the article was heretical, and the first draft of the canon presented to the Council on February 26, 1547, read, "If anyone should say that all Christians have equal power in confecting and administering the Word and the sacraments, A.S." (CT 5, p. 986). The discussion of the Fathers centered principally around the words "equal" and "confecting." Several bishops requested that *parem* ("equal") be deleted so that "there not be insinuated that all Christians have power, though granted not equal."[13] A number of other bishops, however, explicitly stated that they wanted the word to be kept.[14] In the final draft of the canon as it was promulgated by the Council, neither of the contested words was included.

The question that arises out of this discussion is: What sort of "power" was Trent referring to in the canon cited above? Did the Council wish to say that not all Christians have the power of jurisdiction to administer the sacraments? Or was it that not all Christians have that power without which there would be no sacrament? Or was Trent referring to both notions of power? Again, the Council, at least in the context of this particular canon, did not specify exactly what it meant by the words "power in administering the Word and all the sacraments." Canon 10 as promulgated by Trent simply substantiated the authority of the Church to determine the ministers of the Word and sacraments, thereby teaching that only those so designated by the Church can perform these tasks. Whether Trent also understood this general limitation to imply that only those designated by the Church are the ones who have that power without which there could be no sacrament was not clearly resolved by the Council. Considering the interventions of those bishops who expressed opinions about whether or not the modifier *parem* should be retained in the text of the canon, it would appear that there were those who were of the opinion that all Christians do have some power, undetermined though it may be, over the Word and the sacraments. It is only by examining Trent's treatment of the minister of the individual sacraments that it can be seen whether the Council in fact further determined this power.

**Trent and the Minister of Extreme Unction**

The response of Trent to the Lutheran teaching on extreme unction and, in particular, on the proper minister of this sacrament, was discussed in two apparently unrelated sessions of the Council. In 1547, during the time when the Council was being conducted at Bologna, extreme unction was examined along with the articles on the sacraments of orders and matrimony. Four years later, when the Council was moved back to Trent, the sacrament of anointing was completely re-examined along with penance and matrimony. The doctrine and canons that were ultimately promulgated by the Council were the fruit of this latter period of deliberation. In order to gain an accurate understanding of what the mind of the Council was regarding extreme unction, it is necessary that the proceedings of both periods be examined carefully.

*The session of 1547*

Acccording to the *Acta* of the Council, not all the bishops were in attendance at the sessions held at Bologna. One of the Council presidents made an intervention recommending that pressure be brought to bear on those absent bishops so that they would attend and restore full membership to the Council.[15] While the general of the Dominicans expressed hesitancy over the propriety of the Council's continuing with its work until bishops from all the nations were present, it was eventually agreed upon to continue, and the attention of the Fathers turned to the sacraments of extreme unction, orders, and marriage. The theologians were to examine the Reformation teaching on these sacraments so that an appropriate set of canons could be drawn, discussed, and eventually promulgated as the official response of the Church.

### 1. The examination of the theologians

Two articles of Reformation teaching on extreme unction were submitted to the theologians for their investigation. Article 1 disputed the sacramentality of extreme unction:

> Extreme unction is a human invention or a rite received from the Fathers different from the sacraments which have a mandate of God and a promise of grace (CT 6, p. 96).

The second article was an outright condemnation of the practice of the Church:

> Extreme unction is not practiced by the Roman Church according to the position of the Gospel and James; thus the rite is to be changed (CT 6, p. 96).

Thus the primary focus of the Council's deliberations was on the Reformers' position regarding the nature and origin of the rite of extreme unction as well as on their accusation that the Church had abused its authority in practicing this ritual in a way contrary to the Marcan and Jacobean texts.

The *Acta* note several specific writings from which these articles were drawn. Regarding the source for article 1, Luther's *Babylonian Captivity* and article 13, chapter 6, "De numero et usu sacramentorum," of the *Apologia Confessionis Augustanae* (1531) of Melancthon were cited. Although much of the actual wording of the article submitted to the Council was taken from the *Apologia*, the rendering omitted the phrase "which not even the Church requires as necessary for salvation."[16] This omission could be attributed simply to the fact of unfamiliarity with the actual text of the *Apologia*. It may also have been because the oblique reference to the authority of the Church contained in the deleted phrase could have been misconstrued as an admission on the part of the Church of the lesser importance of extreme unction and confirmation. Since the authority of the Church was central to the sixteenth-century debate over the sacramentality and practice of extreme unction, it may have been judged expedient to omit any reference to that authority which might be misinterpreted as evidence weakening the Church's teaching on anointing.

Concerning the second article, the *Acta* note an accurate citation from Luther's writings which explained the sense according to which a ritual anointing with oil could have value.[17] General reference to Calvin's *Institutes*, chapter 19, and Melancthon's *Loci communes theologici*, completes the listing of the specific sources for article 2.

The theologians approached the question of the sacramentality of extreme unction in several ways. First, the two principal Scripture texts, Mark 6:13 and James 5:14-15, were discussed. On the basis of the Marcan passage, many of the theologians attempted to identify concretely the act of sacramental anointing with Christ and thereby substantiate its divine institution and consequent sacramentality. The discussion that ensued indicates that they were cognizant of the medieval debate over the mode of institution of extreme unction, and caution was urged not to look hastily to Mark as evidence for direct institution.[18] Others cited James 5:14-15 as evidence that extreme unction is a sacrament. According to them, since the text of James notes that grace is given and sins are taken away as a result of this anointing, the rite had to be instituted by Christ, since no human being has the power to institute a rite that could produce these effects.[19]

The second method of argumentation in support of the sacramentality of extreme unction rested upon the official teaching authority of the Church as exercised in earlier councils. The most frequently cited conciliar document was the *Decree for the Armenians* of the Council of Florence. Other conciliar documents noted by the theologians included canons 76-78 of the Fourth Council of Carthage; the bull *Inter cunctas* of the Council of Constance;

canon 43 of the Third Council of Carthage; canons 47-48 of the Council of Laodicea; and the First and Second Councils of Toledo.[20] A careful examination of these conciliar references casts a shadow on the accuracy of these theologians' citations. Canon 43 of the Third Council of Carthage has nothing to do with the sick. Canons 76-78 of the Fourth Council of Carthage deal with the reconciliation of sick penitents but make no specific mention of extreme unction or any rite of anointing. Finally, the canons of the fourth-century Council of Laodicea refer to the reception of baptism by a sick person and mention an anointing that dubiously points to extreme unction.[21]

The theologians also drew an argument from a limited number of the writings of the Fathers and theologians on extreme unction. The most common documents cited were the letter of Pope Innocent I to Decentius, the commentary of Theophylact on Mark 6:13, and Augustine's *De visitatione infirmorum*.[22] Although the papal letter indisputably identifies the sacramental anointing of the Church with that prescribed by James, the value of the commentary of Theophylact is questionable. It has already been demonstrated that the *De visitatione infirmorum*, which is generally accepted today as being of later authorship and falsely attributed to Augustine, simply numbers the anointing referred to in James among the sacraments and describes it as a "typical unction of the Holy Spirit."[23]

Concerning the second article, which generically rejected the Church's practice of extreme unction as being contrary to the Scriptures, the theologians responded by making more specific observations regarding the administration of the sacrament only to those *in extremis* and the use of consecrated oil and a deprecative form, which practices the Reformers had cited as examples of how the Church had abused its authority.

While many of the theologians spoke directly about the effects of extreme unction, only two are recorded as having addressed the proper subject of the sacrament. Jeronimo of Salamanca stated that the anointing should not be given to just any sick person desirous of grace. Pietro Januarius was even more specific. He refuted the view that the Apostles anointed all the sick, basing his argument on "the use of the Church which was taught by them [the Apostles] as is seen in the Council of Florence, which asserts that those close to death are to be anointed."[24]

The theologians defended the Church's use of consecrated oil and a deprecative form simply by stating that the Reformers' position was contrary to that of the Church, and in so teaching they were accusing the Church of having erred. As Jeronimo of Salamanca said:

> The Roman Church has always held that extreme unction is a true sacrament; therefore he who speaks contrary sins against the Holy Spirit. And if anyone should say that the Roman Church has erred, he would make Christ a liar, who promised that he would be with the Church until the consummation of time; for if [the Church] had erred, Christ was not with it. But it is impossible that the Church err; therefore that which is held by it is to be taken as the truth (CT 6, p. 103).

This position was confirmed by Giovanni Battista Moncalvius:

> All the articles proposed are heretical, both on extreme unction as well as on orders and marriage, for the principal reason that they are against the understanding and consensus of the holy Church. For he is a heretic who alienates himself from the holy Catholic Church (CT 6, pp. 117-118).

Several observations arise from the deliberations of the theologians. First of all, nowhere in their discussion of the second article was any explicit mention made of the minister of this sacrament being only the priest, even though this restriction was clearly cited by the Reformers as further evidence of how the Church had abused the sacrament. Furthermore, the theologians claimed that the Protestant articles were heretical, not because their content opposed divine revelation, but because the teaching was contrary to the understanding and practice of the Church. Therefore, even though some of them assigned to one or the other article the theological note "false,"[25] they were unanimous in their decision that both articles should be condemned as heretical because they were against the understanding of the Church. As the *Acta* note:

> All the articles proposed are considered to be condemned as heretical, false and erroneous, and against the understanding and consensus of the Catholic Church (CT 6, p. 121).

## 2. *The deliberations of the Council Fathers in general session*

According to the *Acta* of the Council, the general convocation of bishops considered two canons regarding extreme unction.

> 1. If anyone should say that extreme unction of the sick which James, the Apostle of Christ, in his canonical epistle, commended to the faithful is not a true sacrament instituted by our Lord himself but (either) a certain rite accepted from the Fathers or (and thus) a human figment as if it did not have the mandate of God nor a promise of grace, A.S.
>
> 2. If anyone should say that the use of holy extreme unction has not been perpetually observed in the Catholic Church from the time of the institution by Christ and promulgation of the Apostles or can be disregarded by the faithful without sin, A.S. (CT 6, pp. 308-309).

According to these canons, the bishops wished to defend three basic positions regarding extreme unction. First, extreme unction is a sacrament, instituted by Christ. Because it has those conditions necessary for being a sacrament as delineated by the Reformers, that is, a divine mandate and a promise of grace, this anointing cannot be considered to be a rite of human origin. Second, there is an identity between the anointing practiced by the Church and that instituted by Christ and promulgated by the Apostles. Third, having established this identity, the Church has the right to impose upon the faithful the acceptance of extreme unction as a sacrament which if disregarded would incur the pain of sin.

One of the major points of discussion regarding canon 1 centered around the name to be used in referring to this sacrament. Several of the bishops did not want it to be called "extreme unction," primarily because this designation was not used by Mark or James.[26] Others, however, explicitly indicated that they wished that the name be retained, since that is how the doctors of the Church had referred to it. Moreover, it is the title the Reformers used as an argument to attack the Church. Thus the Servite general, Agostino Bonuccio, explained:

> It is called "extreme" not because it cannot be repeated, but because it is given *in extremis* and because it is the last in respect to the other sacraments.[27]

A number of the Fathers cited Mark 6:13 as evidence of the institution of extreme unction by Christ, thereby establishing its divine origin.[28] There was considerably more discussion, however, concerning the role played by James. Several bishops suggested that the canon should indicate that the anointing was "promulgated" by James.[29] Others seemed to be hesitant to use the word "promulgate" because there had been so much development regarding the sacrament since the time of James. Recognizing that the Church had the authority to expand upon and even change certain aspects of this sacrament which were considered to be of apostolic promulgation, Angelo Pasquale, the bishop of Motula, recommended that the canon be modified.

> The matter of this sacrament is olive oil blessed by a bishop, which oil at the time of James was not blessed. The form of this sacrament is deprecative, as James indicated; another form was given by Ambrose, which the Church now uses. And if James promulgated it, therefore the Church ought to use only the form of James. In the first canon, therefore, in place of the words, "which James . . ." there should be said, "which James and the Church promulgated" (CT 6, pp. 313-314).

There was further disagreement over the words "a certain rite accepted from the Fathers and thus a human figment" in canon 1. Several bishops were satisfied with the text because they were the words of the Reformers; others suggested that the phrase "and thus" be deleted because of the inaccurate inference that such rites are of human invention (CT 6, pp. 315-316).

The principal debate regarding canon 2 was concerned with whether the text should refer to the "perpetual use" of extreme unction. Reservations were expressed by some Fathers regarding the accuracy of the claim of "perpetual observance." The Servite general in particular noted that there appeared to be evidence that the Church had not always used this sacrament in the same way (CT 6, p. 318).

It was out of this initial discussion of all the Council Fathers that there arose the suggestion made by Tommaso Caselli, the bishop of Bertinoro, that there be included either in canon 2 or in a new canon that the bishop is the "confector" of this sacrament and the priest is the minister (CT 6, p. 316). Not only was this intervention the first concrete suggestion that the Council officially declare the proper minister of extreme unction, but it also seemed to reflect the unique theory present in the Middle Ages, refuted at that time by most theologians but accepted in a certain sense by others, that viewed the consecrated oil as the sacrament.[30]

### 3. *Examination of the canons by the bishop-theologians*

After the general congregation of Council Fathers completed its investigation of the two canons on extreme unction, a special group of bishop-theologians considered the various interventions that had been made. They began by addressing the lack of unanimity among the bishops over the use of the title "extreme unction." Their reasons for retaining the traditional title stemmed not only from the fact that this is the way that the doctors and councils of the past had referred to the sacrament, but also, since the sacramental system relates to each stage of a person's life, this anointing is the sacrament specifically for those about to depart from this life. As such, it is only to be administered to those who are *in extremis,* and as the last anointing given by the Church to the faithful, it is appropriate that it be called extreme unction.

Benedetto de' Nobili, the bishop of Accia, seems to have been the only bishop-theologian who took exception to calling the sacrament extreme unction. He was uncomfortable with this title, not just because it is not found in the Scriptures but also because the Church had not always in the past restricted this anointing to those *in extremis*. At the same time, however, he stated that he was in agreement with the present discipline of the Church in anointing only the dying so that they be prepared for glory (CT 6, pp. 328-329). In accepting this restriction, Bishop de' Nobili recognized that the Church had the authority to so modify the practice of this sacrament.

The question of the name to be used for this anointing was finally resolved when Cardinal del Monte, one of the Council presidents, reminded the bishops that since the Fathers had called this sacrament "extreme unction" in canon 1 on the sacraments in general, he could not see how the Council now could refer to it under a new name (CT 6, p. 329).

The bishop-theologians then turned to the question of how the role played by James should be expressed. The argument of those who favored the more specific phrase that extreme unction was "promulgated" by James was summed up by the Servite general, who said that "since there is not found [in the Scriptures] the expressed institution of this sacrament, there is an expressed promulgation in James" (CT 6, p. 342). Those who held that the original word "commended" should be retained pointed to Mark 6:13 as evidence that the Apostles were anointing before James wrote, and they concluded that the other Apostles also promulgated the sacrament orally.[31] They finally agreed to retain the more comprehensive word "commended," which would include both the fact that James promulgated the sacrament and allow that it was also promulgated by the other Apostles, even though there is no explicit scriptural evidence for this fact.

Caution was also expressed about condemning the phrase "a certain rite received from the Fathers," since "rites of the Fathers" was understood to refer to the traditions of the Apostles. Several bishop-theologians were in favor of keeping the words, since the Reformers did not understand these rites to be the traditions of the Apostles but the inventions of other men. They did suggest, however, that the explanatory phrase "and so" ("they are a human figment") be changed (CT 6, p. 342). Others were of the opinion that the entire phrase should be struck from the text because it was not the words of the Reformers.[32] This discussion supports the contention that many of the bishops did not have a first-hand familiarity with all the writings of the Reformers, at least not with article 13 of the *Apologia Confessionis Augustanae*, in which this phrase was contained.

The original canon 1 was amended to read:

> If anyone should say that extreme unction of the sick is not a true sacrament instituted by our Lord Jesus Christ or is not that anointing which James commended in his canonical epistle but only a rite, a certain human invention which does not have a mandate of God nor a promise of grace, A.S. (CT 6, p. 352).

The revised canon 1 retained the name "extreme unction." It also included the simple statement that extreme unction was instituted by Christ, without commenting on the mode of institution or offering a Scripture text as evidence. Moreover, the sacrament was identified with the anointing that James "commended," and the words "rites received from the Fathers" were deleted, even though they are found in the *Apologia*. Finally, specific mention was made of the traditional Reformation conditions for a sacrament, namely, a divine mandate and a promise of grace.

With regard to canon 2, the major discussion of the bishop-theologians centered around how the "use of the Church" in the administration of extreme unction was to be expressed and if it could be said that the present practice has been "perpetually observed." The Council president asked the bishops whether it should be stated that James was speaking of anointing those *in extremis* or any sick person, and if the restriction of this sacrament to the dying was therefore injurious to other sick people (CT 6, p. 353). The majority of those who responded agreed that it should not be declared that James was speaking only of an anointing *in extremis*, since it could not safely be asserted that never was there a time when the Church did not anoint only the dying. Others were of the opinion that even though the primitive Church may have given this sacrament to sick persons who were not laboring *in extremis*, it is sufficient that at the same time the Church also anointed those who were at the point of death. They all concluded, however, that it should be explicitly stated that this restriction is not injurious to the sick.[33]

In an effort to clarify the discussion, the Council president made the following intervention:

> Some Fathers wish to declare that this use of anointing those *in extremis* was always in the Church to such a degree that never were people anointed except those laboring *in extremis;* and this is of great importance, since it cannot easily be proved and seems dangerous to claim that never was there a time when some sick people were anointed who were not *in extremis* and that the Church has always anointed the dying, even the primitive Church. It is permitted that today only the dying are anointed, even though it cannot be denied that James and Mark speak generically (CT 6, p. 359).

Nevertheless, several Fathers continued to insist on the need for determining that the Church had always anointed only the dying, for if extreme unction is a sacrament, it was always a sacrament and could only be given to the dying. Otherwise, as Cornelio Musso observed, "extreme unction as extreme would not be a sacrament, which is false. Therefore, the Church could not give it at any time except to the dying" (CT 6, p. 359). The impasse was resolved when several bishops expressed the opinion that it was not necessary to determine that the anointing was always given to the dying, since the canon seemed to say enough to condemn the heretics without making a claim that would be difficult to verify historically.

The final form of canon 2 approved by the bishops read:

> If anyone should say that the holy and salutary use of extreme unction has not always been observed in the Catholic Church from the time of the institution of Christ and apostolic promulgation or that it yields to an injury of the sick person that this anointing is conferred only on those whose death is feared or denies that its effect is the cure of the mind and in so far as it is advantageous to the soul, also of the body, A.S. (CT 6, p. 365).

The revised canon 2 retained the claim of the constant use of extreme unction by the Church, although the word used was "always" rather than "perpetually." Moreover, there was included, as requested, the specific assertion that the restriction of the administration of extreme unction only to the dying is not injurious to the other sick persons. No mention was made that the words of James were to be understood as referring only to the dying or specifically that the restricted use of the Church has been observed from the time of the primitive Church.

It was during the discussion on canon 2 that two of the bishop-theologians requested that the confector and the minister of the sacrament also be declared "so that all the heresies of the Lutherans can be gotten rid of, since they interpret *inducat presbyteros* as *seniores,* not as priests."[34] In keeping with this suggestion, the Council president submitted a third canon for the deliberation of the bishop-theologians:

If anyone should say that the minister of extreme unction is not the priest alone or that the sacrament can be conferred by any oil other than that which the bishop blesses, A.S. (CT 6, p. 358).

While the majority of the bishop-theologians approved of the canon as it stood, several of the Fathers questioned whether it was necessary. De Nobili did not feel there was a need to make any mention of the minister of this sacrament because this had already been determined by Pope Innocent III (CT 6, p. 365). Ambrosius Pelargus, the Dominican procurator, likewise considered the canon unnecessary because the Lutherans were principally denying that this anointing was a sacrament. Furthermore, he observed, since they did not use "priests" nor blessed oil, they need not be responded to by this canon (CT 6, p. 365). The final decision of the bishop-theologians was to submit a canon on the minister and matter of extreme unction, and with a few minor changes the original text was retained.

4. *Observations regarding the deliberations of the session of 1547 on extreme unction*

A number of observations can be made regarding the deliberations of the 1547 session of the Council, which led to the promulgation of three canons on extreme unction. Although it was recognized that many of the bishops of the Church were not in attendance, nowhere in the *Acta* of this session is there any indication that the Fathers present at Bologna were not conscious of the fact that they were carrying on the official work of the Council. Their major concern was to respond to the Reformers' rejection of extreme unction as a sacrament of the Church and their claim that the Church in its practice of this sacrament had deviated from the instruction of James. It was only as the discussion proceeded that the Council became concerned with the more specific issues such as the matter, form, effects, and minister of the sacrament. Only then did the suggestion arise regarding a specific statement that the priest is the proper minister of the sacrament. Clearly, this question was not a primary concern in the beginning.

With regard to the arguments used both by the theologians and the bishops, Mark 6:13 and James 5:14-15, the two texts traditionally accepted as being in some way related to extreme unction, were frequently referred to only in a general way. Although many of the Fathers seemed to recognize that the Marcan text bore a vague reference to extreme unction, it was interesting to see, in the light of the clarity of James 5, their hesitancy to attribute to James the function of being the promulgator of anointing. While the theologians, and to a lesser degree the bishops, made use of conciliar and ecclesiastical documents as authoritative sources in proving especially the sacramentality of extreme unction, they referred only to a limited number of texts and oftentimes cited documents that remain questionable as to their direct bearing on extreme unction.

Perhaps the strongest reason mentioned in the Council deliberations for rejecting the Reformers' teaching was that it was contrary to the understanding and custom of the Church. As a result, a number of bishops defended the sacramentality of extreme unction simply by making this claim on the basis that the Church had always taught it. According to their mindset, by contradicting this teaching of the Church, the Reformers were accusing the Church of having erred, thereby sinning against the Holy Spirit and subjecting themselves to condemnation. This basic methodology is further confirmed by the observation made about the theologians who, while they assigned varying theological notes to the articles on the three sacraments of orders, marriage, and extreme unction, still judged them all to be worthy of condemnation. This fact illustrates the broad understanding of the notions of "heresy" and "*anathema sit*" that was prevalent at the time of the Council.

The authority of the Church was also the underlying issue in the discussion of the Fathers regarding the perpetual observance of extreme unction. The bishops were aware of many of the historical determinations and changes this sacrament had undergone, and yet they were able to claim that the Church had always observed extreme unction since the time of its institution. In so doing, they accepted these developments as examples of the Church exercising its legitimate authority over the sacraments.

The clearest evidence of the competence of the Church to make a change in this sacrament emerged in the discussion of whether the name "extreme unction" could be retained in defending the perpetual observance of the Church. The question that was extensively debated by the Fathers was: Does the claim of perpetual observance mean that there was never a time when the Church did not anoint only the dying? The use of the title "extreme unction" seemed to imply that there was never such a time. Nonetheless, most of the bishops admitted that it would be most difficult to substantiate such a claim, especially in light of the general references to the sick in Mark and James. According to the opinion that prevailed, even though this anointing was given, at least in the primitive Church, to a sick person who was not *in extremis*, it sufficed to justify the claim of perpetual observance as long as there were some persons among those who were anointed who in fact were *in extremis*.

When canon 2 is read in the light of this discussion, it is clear that there is implied in this definition an acknowledgment on the part of the Council of the Church's competency to restrict the administration of extreme unction, even though the bishops were aware that this restricted use was a development beyond apostolic times. Trent understood that the Church could impose this restriction as authoritative. According to the mentality of the Council, the denial of this restricted use by the Reformers was worthy of condemnation, not because the restriction was of apostolic determination but because it was a rejection of the authority of the Church to make such a change.

Finally, it was noted that canon 3, which contained the specific reference to the minister of the sacrament, received only a cursory examination by the bishops. Initially the suggestion calling for this canon included the puzzling distinction between the bishop as confector of the sacrament and the priest as minister. This distinction gave way to a statement on the oil blessed by the bishop as being the sacramental matter, and the priest as being the minister of anointing. Although several bishops questioned the need for the canon, it was decided to promulgate it as a further defense of the Church's practice regarding this sacrament.

*The session of 1551*

A typhus epidemic was the occasion for the transfer of the Council in 1547 from Trent to Bologna. The move carried with it political overtones, for the city of Trent was under the influence of Emperor Charles V, while Bologna was under papal hegemony. The decree of transfer issued by Pope Paul III was protested by fourteen bishops, most of whom were subjects of the Emperor, and they remained in Trent. Although the Council had proceeded as officially convoked with the majority of the Fathers present, the material treated at Bologna, including that concerning extreme unction, could not be adopted by the Pope, who feared that it would push to the breaking point the tension with Charles that had resulted from the transfer of the Council. He initially rejected the Emperor's demand for the return of the Council to Trent, but after Charles submitted a solemn protest both in Rome and in Bologna, Pope Paul III decreed the suspension of the Council's deliberations on February 16, 1548. Paul's successor, Julius III, yielded to the pressure of the Emperor, and on November 14, 1550, he decreed that the Council be moved back to Trent. It was determined that the Council's deliberations on extreme unction, among other subjects, were to be repeated.

1. *The articles of Reformation teaching*

Four articles containing the heretical teaching of the Reformers concerning extreme unction were presented along with articles on penance. The first was concerned with the sacramentality of extreme unction and was similar to the first article proposed in 1547. The second article, although not included in the earlier Council session, contained a development of the Lutheran rejection of extreme unction as a sacrament:

> Extreme unction not only does not confer grace or the remission of sins, nor does it alleviate the sick who at one time were cured through the grace of cures, and so this anointing ceased with the primitive Church, as did the grace of cures (CT 7, p. 239).

The third article was reminiscent of article 2 of the previous session and disavowed any identification between the present use of anointing by the Church and the anointing recommended by James. It claimed that the practice of the Church should be changed and that the anointing can be disregarded by the people without any moral blame. The final article dealt specifically with the minister of extreme unction:

> The minister of extreme unction is not the priest alone; the presbyters of the Church whom blessed James instructed are to be brought in to anoint the sick are not the priests ordained by the bishop, but those who are older in any community (CT 7, p. 240).

The sources cited by the *Acta* for this article are Melancthon's *Loci communes*, his *Apologia*, and chapter 19 of Calvin's *Institutes*. It should be noted, however, that nowhere did Melancthon specifically state anything about the Church allowing only priests to administer extreme unction. Furthermore, although Calvin commented in chapter 19 of the *Institutes* on the Church's interpretation of the elders in James as being "sacrificing priests," it was Luther, in his *Babylonian Captivity*, who exegeted the Jacobean passage in words almost identical to those used in the article. There is no indication in the *Acta*, however, of the *Babylonian Captivity* as a source of this article.[35]

When these articles are compared with those of 1547, it is evident that the second listing was more expansive than that discussed four years earlier. Unlike the earlier set, mention was made from the very beginning of the effects of anointing, whether or not it can be disregarded by the faithful, and, most importantly, the minister of extreme unction. Furthermore, implied in the fourth article on the minister of anointing was an attack on the authority of the Church, not only because of its interpretation of the words of James as indicating ordained priests but also in restricting this administration only to priests ordained by a bishop.

## 2. *The investigation of the theologians*

The theologians began their investigation of these articles along with those on penance on October 20, 1551, and concluded their study ten days later. According to the *Acta*, out of a total of thirty-six theologians who spoke to the combined list of articles on penance and extreme unction, only seven directed any specific comments on the four articles related to anointing. Those who did discuss these articles directed most of their remarks to the first article on the sacramentality of extreme unction.

While several of the scholars cited Mark 6:13 as substantiating the sacramentality of extreme unction, others accepted the anointing mentioned therein as a prefiguring or foreshadowing of the sacrament.[36] These same theologians commented on James 5:14-15. In their opinion, not only does the text define James' role as being that of promulgator, but it also illustrates the sacramentality of the anointing because it refers to an external sign and ceremony in which sins are remitted and grace is conferred, thereby identifying all the things necessary for a sacrament.[37] The theologians also noted only a limited number of non-biblical sources. Among those cited, in addition to the letter of Innocent I, they referred to the *De visitatione infirmorum*, the commentary of Theophylact on Mark 6:13, the *Quum venisset* of Innocent III, and Chrysostom's *De sacerdotio*, all of which are questionable as to their pertinence to extreme unction.[38]

When it came to defending the contemporary practice of the Church, the theologians simply stated that all the elements specified by James were present. No mention was made of the restricted administration of extreme unction to the dying, which was at the heart of the Reformers' rejection of the Church's practice. Finally, citing the argument of Thomas Aquinas that the nature of the prayer in extreme unction requires that it be made in the person of the Church, they rejected the fourth article because this kind of prayer belongs only to the priest (CT 7, p. 286).

The only theologian who appeared to take a different stand with regard to the fourth article was Diego Chiavez, a Spanish Dominican. Although he inaccurately attributed a citation from the letter of Innocent I to Luther,[39] he interpreted the Lutheran use of this papal document as evidence for the possibility of any Christian to anoint. Thus he observed: "It is licit in the case of a necessity, but then this anointing would not be a sacrament, just as confession made before a layman in the case of necessity is not" (CT 7, p. 281).

Chiavez did not state the source for his claim. It may have been a simple application of the Scholastic debate on whether or not confession to a lay person is considered to be sacramental, or perhaps a reference to the position taken by the theologians Gerald of Cambrai (12th century) and Thomas Waldensis (15th century), each of whom explicitly stated that in the case of necessity a lay person could anoint. Gerald had cited Innocent I as his source. Waldensis depended on Bede's commentary on James, wherein Bede admits to the possibility of lay anointing, although no mention is made of the case of necessity as being a prerequisite. What is significant, however, is that an explicit mention of lay anointing on the authority of Pope Innocent I was made at the Council, even though this anointing was not considered to be a sacrament.

### 3. *Examination of the articles by the Council Fathers*

When the general congregation of the Council Fathers turned their attention to the articles on penance and extreme unction, the *Acta* note that the observations which had been made by the theologians had not been distributed to the bishops because, "they were of little importance and to save time" (CT 7, p. 292). Thus the comments on the eight articles about penance were read to the assembly. There is no record, however, that any of the observations made by the theologians on extreme unction were ever presented to the bishops.

Whereas the general congregation discussed the articles on penance quite extensively, offering theological arguments and authoritative sources from both conciliar and non-conciliar documents, their discussion of the Reformers' teaching on anointing was minimal. Several bishops offered varying reflections on the relationship between Mark 6:13 and James 5:14-15 and the sacrament of extreme unction, and their positions were not dissimilar to those expressed by the theologians. None of the bishops elaborated on the second article.

The only substantive discussion of the third article was the interesting observation of the bishop of Guadix, Martin Ayala:

> The first part of the third article does not seem to be simply condemned because many things have been added for the beauty of the

sacraments concerning their rite which were not observed before, where even now they are observed as pertaining to the substance just as if they were instituted by God (CT 7, p. 316).

Ayala recognized development in the ritual of the sacrament by ecclesiastical determination, some of which was accepted as pertaining to the essence of the sacrament as if it had been determined by Christ, so he was of the opinion that it could not be said that the rite of this sacrament had been observed by the Church in always the same manner as prescribed by James.

Only three bishops made interventions regarding the contents of the fourth article. Georg Flach drew a number of distinctions between the anointing associated with miraculous cures and that of the sacrament:

> The grace of cures differs from this sacrament because in the former, only faith was required; it is true here, but other things are required. The grace of cures was miraculous, this is not; that was received also by the dead, this one only by the living; that one was conferred by all Christians, this only by priests (CT 7, p. 310).

Clearly Flach understood this lay anointing to be charismatic in nature and not sacramental. Pedro Guerrero, the archbishop of Granada, considered the article to be heretical both on the authority of Innocent I and because St. Paul understood "presbyters" to be priests (CT 7, p. 297). Ayala likewise referred to Paul, noting 1 Timothy 4:12 and 14, where Paul calls Timothy, who was a young man, a "presbyter." Thus, according to Ayala, "presbyter" does not simply mean "an older person" (CT 7, p. 314).

With the exception of these comments, the general procedure that the bishops followed regarding the articles on extreme unction was to simply assign theological notes to the different articles and conclude that they were all heretical and to be condemned. The manner in which several of the bishops expressed this, however, is noteworthy. Berardo Bongiovanni, the bishop of Cambrai, stated:

> Therefore all articles on penance are heretical; the same regarding those on extreme unction. Not all the positions are to be condemned in the same way, for some are heretical, others scandalous, some are rash, some false and lying, some presumptuous, some impious

and blasphemous. Which fact ought to be expressed in the preamble of the decree (CT 7, p. 301).

The bishop of Syracuse, Girolamo Bononi, seemed to be of the same opinion:

> Also all the remaining articles both on penance and extreme unction are to be condemned, but not all in the same way but according to their qualities as some erroneous, false, blasphemous, impious, heretical, etc. (CT 7, p. 304).

The bishops of Bassorah and Modena qualified the condemnation in another way: "All the articles proposed are heretical in the meaning of the heretics and are to be condemned by an anathema" (CT 7, p. 318).

A number of the Fathers gave various notes to different parts of the fourth article. Sebastian von Heusenstamm, the archbishop of Mainz, supported by Adolf von Schaumburg and John of Isenburg, considered that the first part of the article ("The minister of extreme unction is not the priest alone") to be *temerarius*, the second part ("and the presbyters whom blessed James exhorted to be brought in to anoint the sick are not priests ordained by a bishop") and the third part ("but those older in age in any community") as erroneous (CT 7, p. 294). Paulo Gregorianz, Friedrich Nausea, and Juan Fonseca all qualified the article as "false" in all parts and stated that it was to be condemned like all the others by an anathema (CT 7, pp. 296, 302).

4. *The deliberations of the Fathers on the canons concerning extreme unction*

Nine Council Fathers were named to formulate the canons and doctrine on penance and extreme unction to be presented to the general congregation. The canons on extreme unction that were submitted read as follows:

> 1. If anyone should say that extreme unction is not truly and properly a sacrament instituted by Christ our Lord (and promulgated by the Apostle James) but only a rite accepted from the fathers or a human invention, A.S.
>
> 2. If anyone should say that the holy anointing of the sick does not confer grace nor remit sins nor alleviate the sick, but has already

ceased in the Church as if it was at one time only a grace of healing, A.S.

3. If anyone should say that the rite and use of extreme unction which the holy Church observes is contrary to the opinion of blessed James the Apostle and therefore is to be changed and can be disregarded by Christians without sin, A.S.

4. If anyone should say that the presbyters of the Church whom blessed James exhorted to be brought in to anoint the sick are not priests ordained by a bishop but the older members in any community so that the (proper) minister of extreme unction is not the priest alone, A.S. (CT 7, pp. 326-327).

With the exception of several minor textual changes, the bishops expressed approval of the canons as they stood.

At the same time, a draft of the doctrinal statement on extreme unction was distributed to the Fathers. The first chapter established the sacramentality of the anointing of the sick as instituted by Christ, insinuated by Mark, and commended and promulgated by James. It noted that from apostolic times the Church has taught the matter, form, proper minister, and effect of the sacrament. The second chapter explained the effects of the sacrament in greater detail. The third chapter stated that the proper minister is the presbyter of the Church, by which title was meant not those who are older or the more eminent in the community, but either bishops or priests properly ordained by bishops. It went on to say that this anointing is to be given to the sick, especially to those who are so dangerously ill that they are considered to be dying (CT 7, p. 326). Chapter 3 concluded by addressing the specific claims of the Reformers as they were presented in the articles:

> Therefore they are to be ignored who teach against the obvious and clear position of James that this anointing is either a human invention or a rite received from the Fathers having neither a divine mandate nor a promise of grace; and those who assert that this anointing has already ceased as if it is to be referred to the grace of healing present only in the primitive Church; and those who say that the rite and use which the holy Roman Church observes in the administration of this sacrament is repugnant to the position of James and therefore is to be changed into another; and finally those who claim that this extreme unction can be disregarded by the faithful without sin. All of these things are most blatantly in conflict with the

clear words of the great Apostle. Actually, the Roman Church, the mother and teacher of all the others, observes nothing other in administering this anointing (insofar as those things which comprise the substance of the sacrament) than what blessed James prescribed. Nor can the contempt of so great a sacrament be without a heinous crime and injury to the Holy Spirit himself (CT 7, pp. 356–357).

The Fathers approved the doctrine on anointing as it was submitted, and on November 25, 1551, the doctrinal statements on penance and extreme unction together with their respective sets of canons were solemnly promulgated.

*Observations on the deliberations of the session of 1551 concerning extreme unction*

Although numerous citations from the *Acta* of the Council demonstrate that in the discussion of both the 1547 and 1551 sessions on extreme unction, the Fathers did not always have an accurate knowledge of the writings of the Reformers, it is equally clear that the Council was most sensitive to its historical purpose, namely, to respond to the Reformation attacks on the sacrament of anointing. Nevertheless, some interesting comparisons can be drawn between the deliberations of each of the sessions.

From the outset, it can be said that the investigation of both the theologians and the bishops in 1547 was marked by greater thoroughness than the more cursory treatment of 1551. Nowhere in the latter session is any reference made to the prior deliberations at Bologna; and it was out of the more superficial investigation that the official teaching of the Church was promulgated.

A number of examples illustrate the respective differences in the approach of the two sessions. First, although the use of the Marcan text as evidence for the institution of extreme unction was questioned both times, the difficulties it presents were elaborated upon more in 1547 than in 1551. Moreover, even though the Church had traditionally placed great emphasis on James 5:14-15 as an authority for extreme unction, many of the Fathers at Bologna were hesitant to refer to James as the promulgator of extreme unction. There seemed to be a sensitivity to account for a direct, universal link between the sacrament of the Church and Christ. According to some bishops, if James were termed the promulgator, it might be implied that there would have been a time at which extreme unction might not have been accepted as a sacrament in some parts of the Church. As a result, canon 1 promulgated in 1547 stated that the sacrament was "commended" by James, and canon 2 retained the teaching that extreme unction was of "apostolic promulgation." By using the more general term "commended," it was implied that while James participated in the task of promulgating, he did not bear the sole responsibility for the promulgation of extreme unction. This concern over the role of James was not apparent in 1551. Although the original draft of canon 1 made no mention of James, the phrase "promulgated by blessed James the Apostle" was added at the suggestion of several bishops without any discussion.[40]

The session of 1547 discussed at great length how the Council was to defend the Church's perpetual observance of extreme unction. The difficulty concerned not only the developments in the ritual of the sacrament but especially the Church's practice of anointing only the dying, which restriction appeared to be of ecclesiastical origin. The admitted inability to demonstrate with certitude that the Church has always anointed only the dying made a number of the Fathers wary of any declaration that the Church has perpetually observed "extreme" unction. Eventually the difficulties concerning both ritual changes and this restriction were resolved, and in the end the earlier session defined that extreme unction has always been observed.

In 1551 several bishops raised concern over ritual development, but this was resolved by clarifying that canon 3 was not claiming that the present ritual was the way James administered the sacrament, but only that the contemporary ritual was in accord with the words of James. The latter session made no effort to justify historically the anointing of only the dying, but simply presupposed the practice as fact and explained the significance of such an anointing for those facing death. Implied in the 1551 position, as was the case in the earlier session, was the recognition of the competency of the Church to make this restriction, even though a precedent for such a restricted practice was not historically verifiable.

The deliberations of the latter session likewise confirm what was noted of the Bologna period concerning the mentality of the Council with which the articles of Reformation teaching were condemned. Where on the one hand it was admitted that the contents of the articles ranged from being heretical, false, rash, erroneous, impious, or blasphemous, on the other hand, in another sense, the articles were all considered to be heretical and to be anathematized. The question that arises is: What is the meaning of that "other sense" according to which all the articles were said to be heretical? The Council recognized that implied in the various articles of Reformation teaching was a contumacious denial of and challenge to the Church's authority to teach or to impose certain practices upon the faithful that were not of immediate divine determination. Therefore, because such teaching was in fact an accusation that the Church had erred, it was considered to be heretical and worthy of condemnation, even though the actual contents of the teaching may not have been a denial of something divinely revealed. Clearly the interventions of the Fathers indicate that the concept "heresy" was by no means understood univocally at the Council of Trent.

The question concerning the minister of extreme unction was clearly of secondary importance at the 1547 session, emerging only later on in the discussion, and both sessions gave it a very cursory investigation. At Bologna only one bishop made an attempt to exegete "presbyter" in James by recommending that the explanatory phrase "that is, a priest," be included in the canon. The suggestion was not adopted. In the latter session the interpretation of "presbyter" was part of the original draft. The only effort at justifying this exegesis was made by the bishop of Guadix on the basis of 1 Timothy 4:12 and 14. While the practice of lay anointing was mentioned several times, in each case this anointing was not considered to be sacramental. When the time came for the bishops to assign theological notes to the article on the minister of extreme unction, a number of them did not classify the contents of the article as heretical. Nevertheless, they unanimously included this article among all the others to be condemned as "heretical."

Canon 4, as it was promulgated on November 25, 1551, states:

If anyone says that the "presbyters of the Church" who James says should be called in to anoint the person who is sick, are not priests ordained by the bishops but the older men of any community, and that the *proper* minister of extreme unction is, consequently, not the priest alone, A.S.

The draft of the canon approved by the bishops did not contain the qualifier "proper." The *Acta* do not note the source of this insertion or the reason why it was added.

Given all these observations regarding the teaching of Trent on extreme unction in general and its position on the minister of the sacrament in particular, some conclusions can now be drawn as to whether or not canon 4 is to be regarded as expressing a dogma of faith, as these terms are understood today. This in turn will determine if this canon should continue to be considered an obstacle to the Church's appointing someone other than the priest as the minister of the sacrament of the anointing of the sick.

*Chapter Nine*

## LET THEM ANOINT THE SICK

Down through the centuries theologians have consistently reflected on the degree of authority the Church has to effect changes in the sacraments without prejudice to whatever Christ instituted or normatively determined, directly or indirectly. Although theology has always held that the sacraments look to Christ for their origin, the debated issue revolves around how many of the essential aspects of each sacrament, which at any time are considered to be necessary for its valid conferral, are specifically of divine determination.

Sacramental theologians today appear to be much more comfortable with this debate than their predecessors of the Middle Ages were. They seem to go so far as to admit that in the case of certain sacraments, it was not until later in the consciousness of the Church that the Church became aware that a particular act was an essential, visible manifestation of its nature as the fundamental sacrament, and therefore to be considered sacramental. Although whatever was determined as normative by Christ or the Apostles is to be accepted as binding for all time, contemporary sacramental theology recognizes that, in most cases, such determinations were rudimentary and required further specification. This later, further specification would have been of ecclesiastical origin, and given changing pastoral situations and the development of doctrine, there is the possibility that at least some of these later determinations could be modified.

This observation is of particular importance when it comes to the sacrament of extreme unction. The evidence of the first sixteen centuries clearly indicates that there were significant developments both in the theological understanding and pastoral practice of the Church with regard to the sacramental anointing of the sick. Since many of these changes were radical in nature and emerged at a time of great disciplinary reform in the Church, especially within the priestly ministry, the history of extreme unction is testimony to the Church's recognizing its authority and competency over the sacraments, giving a more specific form to the sacrament of anointing as certain historical circumstances arose.

This especially seems to be the case regarding the question of who can administer the sacrament of the anointing of the sick. Historically, the restriction of the administration of this anointing to priests dates from the time of the Carolingian Reform in the eighth century. The documents of the preceding centuries clearly indicate not only that the practice of lay anointing was widespread, but that it was regarded as being a sacramental administration, and together with that administered by priests, was the same anointing as prescribed by James. Following the disciplinary action of the Church that restricted the anointing to priests, the lay administration of anointing ceased as a generally accepted practice. In addition, in an effort to further substantiate sacerdotal anointing, there are a number of cases in which the authoritative fifth-century letter of Innocent I to Decentius, which testified to the phenomenon of lay anointing, was grammatically altered or, by means of an anachronistic application of the distinction between a sacrament and a sacramental, given a forced interpretation.

These facts must be seen in light of the conclusion of much of contemporary scholarship that views the specifically "priestly" connotation of the New Testament office of presbyter and the traditional attribution of sacramental powers to priests alone as the results of a process of development that extended into the third century. It would appear that the limiting of the administration of this sacrament to priests alone was not the result of some apostolic determination, but one of a number of ecclesiastical modifications the Church made regarding the sacramental anointing of the sick, due at least in part to the theological understanding and the pastoral needs of the time.

In more recent centuries, however, the principal obstacle to concluding that the Church could change what it had once determined regarding the minister of this sacrament has been the definition of canon 4 of the Council of Trent on extreme unction. Traditionally this canon, which states that only the priest is the proper minister of extreme unction, has been accepted as a defined dogma of faith. In light of the history of this sacrament and the development of the Church's sacramental theology prior to Trent, the deliberations of the Council of Trent regarding sacramental institution, the minister of the sacraments, and extreme unction have been carefully examined, not only to explicate its teaching but also to determine the concerns of the Council when it promulgated, in particular, canon 4.

The immediate context for the Council's teaching on extreme unction was the Reformers' inclusion of the sacramental anointing of the sick among those sacraments that they rejected, primarily because of their inability to locate any direct evidence from the Scriptures that these rituals had been given an express mandate and a promise of grace by the Lord. Implicit in the Reformers' position was the question of the authority of the Church. They accused the Church of having abused its authority both in accepting certain rites as sacraments and by instituting modifications in the practice and celebration of the sacraments.

In response, Trent reasserted the divine origin of all the sacraments. While many at the Council were aware of the medieval debate over the mode of sacramental institution by Christ, Trent simply defined the fact that each of the sacraments had been instituted by the Lord, without determining whether in the case of each sacrament this was a direct or indirect institution. Furthermore, the Council Fathers defended the competence of the Church to make any changes in sacramental matters that did not affect the "substance of the sacraments." Unfortunately, since Trent was silent on the specific mode of sacramental institution by Christ, it almost necessarily had to be silent on exactly what was meant by the phrase "the substance of the sacraments." As a result, the Council offered no more than a generic understanding of this "substance" as being that over which the Church has no competence to initiate change.

This problem of ecclesiastical competence surfaced again in the formulation of Trent's teaching on Communion under both kinds. In this discussion, while the majority of the Fathers held that the Church's authority stopped at whatever was said to be of divine law, there were those who were of the opinion that the Church was capable of changing matters that were regarded as "institutions" and, in the mind of several bishops, even "precepts" of divine law. In each of these cases, these bishops understood that whatever determination the Church made was considered to be perfectly valid and binding. Nevertheless, the general congregation of the Council left unresolved the exact relationship between the authority of the Church and divine law.

Concerning the general question of the minister of the sacraments, although the Lutherans rejected the sacrificial priesthood of the Roman Church, in the interest of good order they all seemed to insist on the need for a public ministry. Thus the Reformers, including Martin Luther, who had specifically stated that all Christians have power over the sacraments, were careful to note that, except in the case of an emergency, only those duly authorized were to proclaim the Word and to administer the sacraments. Trent replied to this position in canon 10 on the sacraments in general by determining that not all Christians have the power to administer the sacraments. Again, however, the Council did not specify exactly what it meant by the word "power," and it cannot be determined whether it was referring to what today would be called the "power of jurisdiction," or to that power without which there can be no sacrament, or to both powers.

While Trent left a number of key questions unanswered, it did make a strong statement that the Church has competence over the sacraments, even though the precise limits of this competence were not drawn. Moreover, implied in the deliberations of the Council, especially concerning Communion under both kinds, was a clear defense of the present structures of the Church as being an incorporation of God's salvific will toward his people, here and now. Trent's intent was not to determine whether or not such structures could be changed, but, true to its historical purpose, to respond to the Lutherans who were rejecting these structures.

With regard to extreme unction, the Reformers had included it among those rites of the Church that they could not accept as sacraments. In addition, because the Church anointed only those who were *in extremis*, they concluded that the Church had abused its authority and had erred by so restricting this ritual, in apparent contradiction to the words of James, which the Church itself accepted as the authoritative basis for this sacrament. The Church's use of only consecrated oil and of a deprecative form and its allowing only priests to anoint were for them further examples of this abuse of authority.

Extreme unction was discussed at two different sessions of the Council of Trent—first in 1547 at the session held in Bologna, and then again in 1551, when the proceedings returned to the city of Trent. In 1547 the Council Fathers initially set out to reassert the sacramentality of extreme unction and to defend, in particular, the Church's practice of anointing only the dying. Some of the bishops seemed to view this restriction as pertaining to the very definition of this sacrament, while others admitted that it lacked historical foundation. The final decision of the session of 1547 to defend the restriction while at the same time not declaring that it had been the constant practice of the Church from the time of Christ, principally because it seemed doubtful that such an assertion could be made with certitude, would appear to be a clear acknowledgment on the part of the Council that the Church had the appropriate authority to make this restriction.

An equally important methodological insight arose out of the proceedings of both sessions that discussed extreme unction. It is evident from the interventions of the bishops who spoke on this sacrament that the Council was aware that it could condemn as "heretical" teachings not unanimously held to be heresy in the sense of being a denial of revealed truth. The basis for the condemnation was that the position of the Reformers, at least as it was understood by Trent, though theologically only false, erroneous, or blasphemous, was contrary to what the Church taught. As such, the Reformation doctrine implicitly accused the Church of having erred in either its teaching or in its practice. Because the Church considered such teaching or practice to be valid and binding for that time, these accusations of error were considered heretical and worthy of condemnation.

The precise question regarding the minister of extreme unction arose only midway during the deliberations on the sacrament in the session of 1547. At the session of 1551, it was presented from the very beginning, but it received little more than a cursory examination. On the basis of what discussion there was, a number of observations can be drawn concerning the Council's treatment of the minister of this sacrament. First, just as the Fathers betrayed a woeful lack of familiarity with the general history of extreme unction, only a few past documents relative to the minister of this anointing were cited. In neither session was a concentrated effort made to verify historically that never was there a time when this sacrament was administered by anyone other than the priest. While several references to the practice of lay anointing were cited, these were summarily dismissed as examples of a non-sacramental use of oil.

Little effort was made to substantiate an interpretation of the "presbyters" in James as "priests." The Council's position on the minister of anointing seemed to be a logical conclusion of its overall defense of the priestly ministry of the Church. While a number of bishops assigned varying theological notes to the contents of the article concerning the minister of extreme unction, they all agreed that the article should be considered "heretical" and be condemned. All these factors would seem to indicate that the primary intention of the Council was to defend the rightful authority of the Church to restrict the administration of this anointing only to priests. According to the mind of the Council, such a restriction, not unlike that whereby extreme unction was to be conferred only to those *in extremis*, was perfectly within the competence of the Church.

To deny this competence pertinaciously would be to accuse the Church of having erred, and this denial would be looked upon as "heretical" and worthy of being anathematized.

On the basis of these observations, it is possible to conclude that there is no contradiction between recognizing, on the one hand, that the Church's restriction permitting only the priest to administer extreme unction is of ecclesiastical origin, dating, as historical documents seem to evidence, from the eighth century, and saying, on the other hand, that the Council of Trent defined as heresy the position which holds that the priest is not the sole proper minister of this sacrament. The solution to this apparent contradiction rests on the fact that Trent was teaching out of its broader notion of "heresy" as explained in the presuppositions outlined in chapter 1 and as illustrated in a number of the interventions during the Council's proceedings.

In such a case, therefore, canon 4 on extreme unction would not be considered a "dogma of faith" in the strict sense of those terms as they are understood by the Church today. In other words, the contents of the Tridentine canon should not be accepted as having been "divinely revealed" and taught as such by the Church. The canon would rather represent a reiteration and a confirmation of a determination lawfully initiated by the Church concerning extreme unction, which determination, at the time it was made and especially at the time of Trent, the Church could impose as necessary for a valid administration of the sacrament.

In light of this interpretation of the Tridentine teaching, it can be concluded that canon 4 on the proper minister of extreme unction is not to be considered an obstacle to the Church's appointing someone other than the priest to administer the sacrament of the anointing of the sick. In fact, if the Church did make such a change, always retaining what is necessary in this sacrament in virtue of the institution of Christ or apostolic-ecclesial determination, it would be an official act on a par with that which it made earlier in its history whereby the administration of extreme unction was restricted to priests. The competence and authority of the Church to make such a change would also seem to be in keeping with the

Tridentine conviction regarding the Church's authority in sacramental matters, which authority it so faithfully and consistently defended in the face of the Reformation attacks.

Although theologically it would appear that it is possible for the Church to designate persons other than the priest to administer the sacramental anointing of the sick, the pastoral question remains: Should such a change be made? There is no doubt that one of the most important responsibilities of the Church is that of ministering to the faithful who are sick and infirm. Whereas in the past this ministry was primarily carried on by priests and consisted principally of visitation and the administration of penance, Communion, and, when the patient was near death, extreme unction, today this pastoral care is also being exercised by permanent deacons and commissioned lay ministers. This development is the result not only of an expanded understanding of ministry and a greater commitment to the needs of the sick but also of the Church's recognition that it faces the future with significantly fewer numbers of ordained priests. Consequently, not only does it appear pastorally appropriate, as was suggested in the Introduction, that these nonsacerdotal ministers be able to administer the sacrament of anointing as the culmination of that pastoral care which they are already exercising, but it is one way of responding to the demands that continue to be made on a shrinking presbyterate.

At the same time it is recognized that a certain confusion might result among the faithful if the Church would permit persons other than priests to adminster the sacramental anointing of the sick. It is also pastorally true that illness is not the time when either a patient or those close to the person who is sick should be expected to deal with the additional adjustments that normally follow any change in the sacramental practices of the Church. However, the average Catholic could readily be instructed so as to be comfortable with the administration of this sacrament by a deacon or non-ordained member of a pastoral health care team.

This necessary catechesis would involve the following points. First of all, there must be clear and sensitive explanation that this sacrament no longer carries with it the former, and at times fearful, connotations of being "extreme unction." It is, as it was originally intended to be, a powerful and consoling public act whereby the Church shares its faith with the infirm person and makes present the healing presence of the Lord. As such, both the community and the individual can experience in faith how God reaches out to comfort and strengthen both the spirit and the body of those who, in the crisis of illness, place their trust in him. The faithful should be reminded that it is the sacrament that is of greater importance, not the one who is administering it.

Second, this catechesis should explain that in the early centuries of the Church lay anointing was as common a practice as sacerdotal anointing. People should not be underestimated in their ability to realize that much of what has been the contemporary practice of the Church actually originated not with Christ but at a particular period in the history of the Church and for specific historical reasons. The majority of practicing Catholics have been on the path of reform long enough since Vatican II to accept that much that was in the Church can be, and oftentimes should be, changed so that the saving ministry of the Lord, of which the Church itself is the primary servant, can be continued more effectively. Moreover, people can also be given the assurance that if, in their time of need, they would be more comfortable with what was the former practice of the Church, a priest will be summoned.

In addition, this catechesis should emphasize that regardless of who administers the anointing, it is a liturgical celebration of faith of the entire Christian community. The medievalists were correct in observing that the prayer of the sacraments is a public prayer and should be led by a public person. Today the ontological change that results from ordination to hierarchical orders tends to be understood relationally. Whether ordination is to the presbyteral or diaconal office, the ordained person, by virtue of his permanent commitment and the public call and acceptance of the Church, not only assumes the identity of being a public person in the Christian community but is also recognized as being charged with the responsibility of exercising in the Church's name its official ministry. The presence of the faith community at large is experienced when a priest or a deacon exercises the officially designated ministerial tasks. With regard to the anointing of the sick, all that remains is that the Church, acting perfectly within its competence, extend the administration of this sacrament to the diaconate.

The commissioning of men and women to the lay ministry is different in a number of ways from the ordination of an individual to the official ministry of the Church. Nevertheless, even though the lay ministry is a special exercise of that general ministry all Christians share by virtue of baptism, the lay minister functions in a way distinct from that of the other non-ordained baptized. By virtue of being officially commissioned, it is recognized that these men and women have been specially trained and are competent to exercise a particular designated ministry. Moreover, they serve with the appointment of the Church. Therefore, in a true sense, lay ministers have a special relationship to the broader community, and they function as public persons when ministering.

When a lay person is appointed to serve in a health care institution, he or she is there not as a private individual but in the name of the Church. The patient soon recognizes in the lay minister's presence the prayer and concern of the faith community. If these lay ministers were designated by the Church to sacramentally anoint those persons under their care, it would be clear that they were administering the sacrament on behalf of the Church. In so doing, the sacramental healing presence of Christ would be just as present as when the ritual is performed by an ordained priest.

Given the unique testimony of the history of the sacrament of anointing and, in particular, its minister; an accurate interpretation of the teaching of Trent, which defended the position that only the priest is the proper minister of extreme unction; and the particular pastoral needs of today and of the future, it is the conclusion of this study that the Church not only can but should extend the administration of the sacrament of anointing of the sick to deacons and, when appropriate, to officially commissioned lay ministers. In so doing, the Church will, in an even more powerful way, give witness to that special concern that the Lord Jesus always had for those burdened by the cross of illness. Let them anoint the sick!

# NOTES

## Introduction (pages 1-6)

1. A copy of the paper prepared by Father Palmer in February 1974 was provided by the Office of the Bishops' Committee on the Permanent Diaconate of the National Conference of Catholic Bishops.
2. Article 16 of the General Introduction to *Pastoral Care of the Sick* states: "The priest is the only proper minister of the anointing of the sick." Reference is then made to canon 4 of the Council of Trent. See *Pastoral Care of the Sick: Rites of Anointing and Viaticum* (Collegeville, Minn.: The Liturgical Press, 1983), p. 14.
3. Canon 1: "If anyone says that the sacraments of the New Law were not all instituted by Jesus Christ our Lord; or that there are more than seven or fewer than seven . . . that is, baptism, confirmation, the Eucharist, penance, extreme unction, holy orders, and matrimony; or that any one of these is not truly and properly a sacrament: A.S." (DS 1601).

    Canon 10: "If anyone says that all Christians have the power to preach the word and to administer all the sacraments: A.S." (DS 1610)
4. While the canons on Communion under both kinds were officially promulgated at Session 21 (July 16, 1562), more than ten years after those on extreme unction, the contents of the canons were first discussed in 1547. As was the case with the discussion on extreme unction, it was decided that the matter should be dealt with again after the return of the Council to Trent.

    The discussion was resumed in September 1551, but after receiving word that the Protestants had petitioned to be present at the Council and had specifically requested that this matter not be settled until they arrived, further deliberations were suspended.

    The earlier discussions of the Council Fathers on Communion under both kinds offer significant insights into the mentality of that time regarding the Church's competency over the sacraments.

## Chapter One (pages 7-25)

1. Peter Lombard admitted that all the sacraments receive their efficacy from the passion and death of Christ, but he did not explicitly state that each of the sacraments was instituted by Christ. He was silent on the institution of confirmation, and he claimed that extreme unction was instituted by the Apostles (*Liber IV sententiarum*, d. 23, cap. 3).

    Albert the Great responded to Lombard's claim, saying that human institution does not suffice for the sacraments; Christ himself instituted all the sacraments of the New Law, and this act of institution extended even to the essential aspects of the sacraments (*Commentarii in IV sententiarum*, lib. 4, d. 23, a. 13).

    According to Thomas Aquinas, since the institution of the sacraments pertains to the fullness of power reserved only to the author of the New Law, all the sacraments were instituted by Christ (*Scriptum super sententias*, t. 4, *Liber quartus sententiarum*, d. 2, q. 1, a. 4). Moreover, Christ's act of institution extended to all the essentials, even though there may be no record of such determination in the New Testament (*Summa* III, q. 64, a. 2).

2. Alexander of Hales referred to the origin of all the sacraments back to Christ. In the case of confirmation and extreme unction, he held that they were properly given after the passion, and he concluded that "the Lord instituted these two sacraments through his Apostles" (*Summa*, q. 3, m. 2, a. 3, par. 6).

    With regard to confirmation, he goes even further: "It was instituted on the instinct of the Holy Spirit at the Council of Meaux with regard to the form of the words and the matter to which the Holy Spirit also bestowed the power of sanctifying" (*ibid.*, q. 9, m. 1).

    Alexander's reference to the Council of Meaux is somewhat puzzling, as there can be found only three canons on confirmation from this Council, and they are all disciplinary in nature. Nevertheless, Alexander understood the apostolic imposition of hands referred to in the Scriptures as a figure of confirmation, which figure had been instituted by Christ. In such a way Christ willed and decreed the sacrament signified in the figure and thereby determined the grace of confirmation. Consequently, Alexander was able to trace a connection between the formal institution of confirmation as to its ritual, apparently including even its matter and form, at the Council of Meaux and the will of Christ.

    According to Bonaventure, Christ instituted all the sacraments, but he did so in different ways: ". . . some by confirming, approving, and consummating them, such as matrimony and penance; some by insinuating and initiating, such as confirmation and extreme unction; some by initiating, consummating, and partaking in himself, such as baptism, Eucharist, and order" (*Breviloquium*, pars. 6, cap. 4). This multiple mode of institution by Christ led Bonaventure to recognize the role of the Church and the Holy Spirit in the task of greater determination, especially in the case of confirmation and extreme unction (*In IVum librum sententiarum*, d. 7, a. 1, q. 1; d. 23, q. 2).

Because Bonaventure was so imprecise about the meaning of the various activities he assigned to Christ, the exact content of the act of apostolic institution is unknown, although it would appear that its general task was to make more specific what was insinuated and initiated by the Lord.

3. K. Rahner, *The Church and the Sacraments* (New York: Herder and Herder, 1963), p. 18.
4. *Ibid.*, p. 22.
5. *Ibid.*, p. 41.
6. *Ibid.*, p. 70.
7. E. Schillebeeckx, *Christ the Sacrament of the Encounter with God* (London: Sheed and Ward, 1963), p. 141.
8. *Ibid.*, pp. 153-154.
9. R. Brown, *Priest and Bishop: Biblical Reflections* (New York: Paulist Press, 1970), p. 17.
10. There are a number of reasons given to explain why the New Testament avoids calling Christian ministers "priests." First, since the title "priest" was too closely associated with the Jewish priests and their cultic functions at the time of the New Testament, any confusion or identification of the Christian ministry with that of contemporary Jewish or pagan priesthoods was avoided by not referring to the ministers of the Church as priests. See D. Donovan, *The Levitical Priesthood and the Ministry of the New Testament* (Münster, 1970).

Moreover, Brown (*op. cit.*, p. 16) questions whether in New Testament times the Eucharist, in spite of the sacrificial overtones present in the traditional words of institution, was considered principally as sacrifice. If in fact the Eucharist was not looked upon as being primarily a sacrifice, there would be no basis for assuming that the early Christians would have considered the one who presided at the Eucharistic meal to be a "priest."

Finally, Donovan (*op. cit.*, pp. 579-580) also suggests that there were a number of factors more sociological than theological in nature that gave rise to the situation in which an analogy could be drawn between the specific offices of ministry that arose in the Church and the priesthood of the Old Testament. Those factors included the stress on unity in the face of the factions that began to appear within the

Christian community, the influence of the Roman preoccupation with order, and the need for strong leadership at the time of persecution. Given these factors, coupled with the growing awareness of the Church as the New Israel and the centrality of the Eucharist in its life, it became only natural that eventually its leadership, which dramatically expressed itself in the Eucharistic and other cultic assemblies, should come to be understood as analogous to the Old Testament priesthood.

11. Donovan, *op. cit.*, p. 117.
12. 1 Timothy 3:1ff. states that the *episkopos* presides over the Christian community; 1 Timothy 5:1, 7 says the same of the presbyters. Titus 1:9 acknowledges that the presbyter must be knowledgeable in doctrine not only for teaching but also for safeguarding tradition. The proper virtues for both the *presbyteros* and the *episkopos* are described analogously (1 Tim 3:1ff.; Titus 1:5ff.), and, in at least the latter reference from Titus (1:7), the title *episkopos* is substituted for *presbyteros* as if they were interchangeable.
13. H. Küng, *The Church* (New York: Sheed and Ward, 1967), pp. 399–400.
14. Other authors think that this explanation may be too simplistic. They question whether the Christian *episkopos* is solely of Hellenistic origin and totally devoid of any Jewish influence. This hesitancy stems from a recent discovery regarding the Qumran community, where the community leader was called *mebaqqer* or *paqid*. Brown notes that the roots of these two Hebrew titles are translated by the Septuagint in various forms of the Greek verb *episkopein*. Moreover, the documents indicate that the function of the *mebaqqer* was that of a supervisor who was responsible not only for the community property but also for the selection and instruction of candidates in the Law of Moses.

    If the Christian *episkopos* and the *mebaqqer* of Qumran are related, the *episkopoi* of Philippians 1:1 may not be as solely Gentile in origin as Küng and others maintain. Brown, *op. cit.*, pp. 67–68; see also M. Bourke, "Reflections on Church Order in the New Testament," *Catholic Biblical Quarterly* 30 (1968), p. 502.
15. Donovan, *op. cit.*, pp. 254–255.
16. Scholarship is divided over the exact dating of the *Didache*. Some authors, such as Donovan (*op. cit.*, p. 263) place it as early as the end of the first century or the beginning of the second, while others are of the opinion that it dates from the mid-second century. See J. Mohler, *The Origin and Evolution of the Priesthood* (New York: Alba House, 1970), p. 39.
17. Quoted in Mohler, *op. cit.*, p. 40.
18. *Ibid.*
19. Donovan, *op. cit.*, p. 278.

NOTES TO CHAPTER ONE (PAGES 7–25)      159

20. In his letter to the Church at Philadelphia, Ignatius writes: "Be eager, therefore, to use one Eucharist . . . for there is one flock of our Lord Jesus Christ and one cup for union with his blood, one sanctuary as there is one bishop, together with the presbytery and the deacons, my fellow servants . . . so that whatever you do, you do in relation to God." Quoted in Mohler, *op. cit.*, p. 42.
21. "God and Father of our Lord Jesus Christ, look upon this thy servant, and grant to him the spirit of grace and counsel of a presbyter, that he may sustain and govern with a pure heart as thou didst look upon thy chosen people and didst command Moses that he should appoint presbyters whom thou didst fill with thy Spirit whom thou gavest to thy servant. And now, O Lord, grant that there may be unfailingly preserved among us the Spirit of thy grace, and make us worthy that believing, we may minister to thee in simplicity of heart, praising thee." Quoted in Mohler, *op. cit.*, pp. 52–53.
22. Donovan, *op. cit.*, p. 439.
23. *Ibid.*, p. 546.
24. Brown, *op. cit.*, p. 41.
25. C. Peter, "Integral Confession and the Council of Trent," *Sacramental Reconciliation*, Concilium 61 (New York: Herder and Herder, 1971), p. 99.
26. *Ibid.*, p. 100.
27. *Ibid.*, p. 103.
28. C. Peter, "Auricular Confession and the Council of Trent," *The Jurist* 28 (1968), p. 294.
29. R. Aubert, "Church History as an Indispensable Key to Interpreting the Decisions of the Magisterium," *Church History in Future Perspective*, Concilium 57 (New York: Herder and Herder, 1970), pp. 103–107.
30. H. Jedin, "Il Concilio di Trento—Scòpo, svolgimento e risultati," *Divinitas* 5 (1961), p. 359.
31. P. Fransen, "Réflexions sur l'anathème au Concile de Trente," *Ephemerides theologicae Lovanienses* 29 (1953), pp. 668–669. In Fransen's exegesis of the Tridentine formula of canon 7 on marriage, he explains the term *errare* to mean that "the anathema and excommunication pointed exclusively to the statements made by the Reformers that in its juridical practice the Church had, in a 'tyrannical way,' exceeded its competence in the matter of divorce" ("Divorce on the Ground of Adultery—The Council of Trent," *The Future of Marriage as Institution*, Concilium 55 [New York: Herder and Herder, 1970], p. 92). See also C. Peter, "Auricular Confession," *op. cit.*, p. 287.
32. P. Fransen, "The Authority of Councils," *Problems of Authority*, ed. J. Todd (Baltimore: Helicon Press, 1962), p. 57.

33. *Ibid.*, p. 73.
34. Melchior Cano, *De locis theologicis*, in *Melchioris Cani opera*, (Padua: Typis Seminarii, 1734), p. 363.
35. *Ibid.*
36. *Ibid.*, p. 370.
37. *Ibid.*
38. Fransen, "Réflexions sur l'anathème au Concile de Trente," p. 666.

## Chapter Two (pages 26-40)

1. In looking at the New Testament references to the care of the sick, the sending of the seventy disciples (Luke 10:1-2, 8-9) should also be kept in mind.
2. Some scholars attach verse 16 to the text of James referring to extreme unction: "So confess your sins to one another, and pray for one another, and this will cure you; the heartfelt prayer of a good man works very powerfully." See C. Ruch, "Extrême-onction dans l'Ecriture," DTC 5 (1913), cols. 1960-2005; K. Condon, "The Sacrament of Healing," *Scripture* 11 (1959), pp. 33-42; J.H. Ropes, *The Epistle of St. James: Critical and Exegetical Commentary* (Edinburgh: T. & T. Clark, 1961). We do not include verse 16 as part of the Jacobean text because the overwhelming majority of writers throughout history seem to accept verses 14-15 as referring to extreme unction.
3. See the preceding chapter for an analysis of "presbyter" along with the other New Testament offices of ministry.
4. Hilary of Poitiers, *Commentarius in Matthaeum* (PL 9:967).
5. John Chrysostom, *Homiliae XC in Matthaeum* (PG 57:382).
6. Rufinus tells of the holy men Isidore, Macarius the Great, Macarius of Alexandria, Heraclides, and Pambo, who anointed a paralytic "in the name of the Lord." The afflicted person was immediately cured and went home praising God (*Historia ecclesiastica*, lib. 2, cap. 4 [PL 21:511-512]).

    Palladius gives an account of Macarius of Alexandria, who for twenty days anointed a paralytic woman with "holy oil" while praying over her (*The Lausiac History*, trans. R. T. Meyer, Ancient Christian Writers 34 [Westminister, Md.: Newman Press, 1965], p. 61).
7. Rufinus writes of the cure by Ammon of a boy who had the face of a dragon because of diabolic possession. Mention is made of an anointing with oil but not of any prayer (*Liber de vitis Patrum*, cap. 8 [PL 21:421]). He also reports two cures of possessed persons by Macarius the Great, and in each case there is mention of prayer and an anointing "in the name of the Lord" (*ibid.*, cap. 28 [PL 21:451]).

In the Life of St. Pachomius found in the *Acta Sanctorum* (vol. 16, May 14, p. 308), there is an account of a miracle performed for a young man by the holy abbot with the use of "bread and blessed oil."
8. Irenaeus, *Contra haereses*, cap. 21, n. 5 (PG 7:666-667).
9. Tertullian, *Liber de praescriptionibus*, cap. 41 (PL 2:69).
10. Ambrose, *De poenitentia*, lib. 1, cap. 8 (PL 16:497).
11. S. Luff, "The Sacrament of the Sick: A First Century Text," *The Clergy Review* 52 (Jan. 1967), pp. 50–60.
12. Canons 199-200 and 219-222. See L. Duchesne, *Origins of Christian Worship*, trans. M. L. McClure (London: S.P.C.K., 1904), pp. 537–539.
13. Mansi 2, p. 681.
14. Origen, *In Leviticum*, hom. 2, cap. 4 (PG 12:418-419).
15. This opinion is held by authors such as Poschmann, Boudinhon, and Ruch.
16. This is the opinion of Palmer, Bord, and De Sainte-Beuve.
17. John Chrysostom, *De sacerdotio*, lib. 3, n. 6 (PG 48:643-644).
18. Council of Laodicea, *Praefatiuncula*, cap. 7 (Mansi 2, p. 723).
19. Gregory Dix, ed., *The Apostolic Tradition* (London: S.P.C.K., 1937), p. 10.
20. A. Chavasse is of the opinion that the original Greek text contained the word *chriomenois* and that the Latin *utentibus* would be more accurate. According to him, the Ethiopian text, perhaps because of a copyist's mistake, was a translation of *chromenois*, which was rendered "to be anointed." *Etude sur l'onction des infirmes dans l'Eglise latine du $III^e$ au $XI^e$ siècle*, vol. 1: *Du $III^e$ siècle à la réforme carolingienne* (Lyons: Librairie du Sacré Coeur, 1942), pp. 36–37.
21. E. Doronzo, *De Extrema Unctione*, vol. 1 (Milwaukee: Bruce Publishing Co., 1954), p. 108; H. Porter, "The Origin of the Medieval Rite for Anointing the Sick," *Journal of Theological Studies* 7 (1956), pp. 211–225; C. Ruch, "Extrême-onction du $I^{er}$ au $IX^e$ siècle," DTC 5 (1913), col. 1950.
22. See Chavasse, *op. cit.*, pp. 33, 38–39.
23. F. X. Funk., ed., *Didascalia et constitutiones Apostolorum* (Paderborn: F. Schöningh, 1905), pp. 179–181, 191–193.
24. See Ruch, *op. cit.*, col. 1965. J.B. Bord, *L'extrême-onction, d'après l'Epître de saint Jacques, Examinée dans la tradition* (Brussels: Beyaert, 1923).
25. Doronzo, *op. cit.*, pp. 132–133.
26. J. Dauvillier, "Extrême-onction dans les Eglises orientales," *Dictionnaire de droit canonique* 5 (1951-52), pp. 776–777.
27. I. Rahmani, ed., *Testamentum Domini nostri Jesu Christi* (Hildesheim: Georg Olms Verlag, 1968), p. 49.

## Chapter Three (pages 41-57)

1. B. Poschmann gives a unique context to this letter. According to him, Innocent's reply seems to have been occasioned by the excessive claims being made by priests over against bishops regarding control over the sacrament of penance. In other words, since the text of James mentions only presbyters, it was being cited by priests as support for their independence in the administration of penance. Thus Innocent's letter both establishes the correct interpretation of James 5:14-15 as referring to the sick and also addresses the question of the minister of the anointing (*Penance and the Anointing of the Sick*, trans. F. Courtney [New York: Herder and Herder, 1964], pp. 239-241).
2. The controversy arising from the letter of Pope Innocent I centers around the translation of the Latin text given in italics here: "Quod non est dubium de fidelibus aegrotantibus accipi vel intelligi debere, qui sancto oleo chrismatis perungi possunt, quod ab episcopo confectum, *non solum sacerdotibus, sed et omnibus uti Christianis licet in sua aut in suorum necessitate ungendum.*"
3. It should be noted that in saying that this oil is of the "genus of a sacrament," the term "sacrament" did not at that time have the whole significance it would take on with the development of medieval sacramental theology. It is difficult to conclude what more would have been indicated by this term at that time than the fact that this anointing was a holy operation of the Church that would have a beneficial effect on the soul and perhaps the body of the Christian.
4. The Council of Toledo (c. 400) directed that no one other than the bishop can confect "chrism," which is a reference to "blessed oil" and the oil that today is called "chrism" as distinct from the "oil of catechumens" and the "oil of the sick" (Mansi 3, p. 1002).
5. In another letter Pope Innocent replies to a question posed to him by Bishop Exuperius of Toulouse, who was inquiring about the administration of penance and Communion to baptized Christians who had lived incontinent lives and were in danger of death. In his reply the Pope refers to penance and "last Communion" but makes no reference to any rite of anointing (PL 20:498-499).
6. H. Netzer notes that in the Carolingian period an active form of a verb was frequently used in a passive sense ("L'extrême-onction aux VIII et IX siècles," *Revue du clergé français* 68 (1911), p. 184. It should be recalled, however, that the text of Innocent dates from the fifth century and not from the time of the Carolingian period in the late eighth and early ninth centuries.

   J. Kern, in his *Tractatus dogmaticus de sacramento Extremae Unctionis* (Ratisbon: Pustet, 1907), adheres to the active form of the words

but understands them in a passive sense. See also R. Tapper, *Explicationes articulorum venerandae facultatis sacrae theologiae generalis studii Lovaniensis*, vol. 1 (Louvain: M. Verhasselt, 1555), pp. 221–239.
7. J. de Sainte-Beuve, *Tractatus de sacramento Unctionis Infirmorum Extremae*, in Migne, *Theologiae cursus completus* 24 (Paris: Migne, 1841), pp. 43–46; J. Bord, *L'extrême-onction, d'après l'Epître de saint Jacques, Examinée dans la tradition* (Brussels: Beyaert, 1923), p. 103; C. Ruch, "Extrême-onction dans l'Ecriture," DTC 5 (1913), cols. 1954–55; P. de Letter, "Anointing the Sick and Danger of Death," *Irish Theological Quarterly* 29 (1962), p. 294; B. Poschmann, *Penance and the Anointing of the Sick*, trans. F. Courtney (New York: Herder and Herder, 1964), p. 240.
8. A. Chavasse, *Etude sur l'onction des infirmes dans l'Eglise latine du $III^e$ au $XI^e$ siècle*, vol. 1: *Du $III^e$ siècle à la réforme carolingienne* (Lyons: Librairie du Sacré-Coeur, 1942), p. 96; F. Puller, *The Anointing of the Sick in Scripture and Tradition* (London: S.P.C.K., 1904), pp. 55–60; A. Boudinhon, "Si les fidèles se faisaient eux-mêmes autrefois les onctions de l'huile sainte," *Revue du clergé français* 68 (1911), pp. 724–725; C. de Clercq, *Ordre, mariage, extrême-onction* (Paris: Bloud et Gay, 1939), p. 155; A. Villien, "L'extrême-onction," *Revue du clergé français* 70 (1912), pp. 643–644.
9. There are references to James 5:14-15 prior to Bede. Athanasius, in his *Synopsis Sacrae Scripturae*, lib. 4: "Epistolae catholicae septem" (PG 28:406-407) and Cassiodorus, *Complexiones in epistolas Apostolorum*, "Epistola S. Jacobi ad Dispersos" (PL 70:1380), merely give a synopsis of the contents of the Epistle. Somewhat later, John Cassian, in his *Collatio vigesima*, "De poenitentiae fine et satisfactione," cap. 8 (PL 49:1161), reproduces the apostolic instruction as evidence that the prayer of holy people can obtain pardon for sins.
10. Augustine, *De Scriptura Sacra speculum* (PL 34:887).
11. Victor of Antioch, in M. J. Rouët de Journel, ed., *Enchiridion patristicum*, 21st ed. (Freiburg im Breisgau, 1960), no. 2102; J. Cramer, *Catenae Graecorum Patrum in Novum Testamentum*, vol. 1 (Oxford, 1844), p. 340.
12. Bede, *In Marci Evangelium expositio*, lib. 2 (PL 92:187).
13. Bede, *Expositio super Epistolas catholicas: In Epistolam S. Jacobi* (PL 93:39-40).
14. Cyril of Alexandria, *De adoratione in spiritu et veritate*, lib. 6 (PG 68:470-471); John Mandakuni, in J.M. Schmid, *Heilige Reden des Joannes Mandakuni* (Ratisbon, 1871), p. 222.
15. Caesarius of Arles, *Sermones* 13, 50, 52, 184, in G. Morin, ed., *Corpus Christianorum* (Turnhout, 1953ff.), vol. 103, pp. 66–67, 232, 225; vol. 104, p. 751.

16. Eligius, *De rectitudine catholicae conversationis* (PL 40:1172-73).
17. *Codex canonum ecclesiasticorum* (c. 470), cap. 23 (PL 56:518); Dionysius Exiguus (c. 540), *Collectio decretorum Pontificum Romanorum* (PL 84:644); Cresconius, *Breviarium canonicum*, cap. 72 (PL 88:913).
18. *De visitatione infirmorum*, lib. 2, cap. 4 (PL 40:1154). Among the authors who date this document from the ninth century are E. Doronzo, *De Extrema Unctione*, vol. 1 (Milwaukee: Bruce Publishing Co., 1954), p. 149; and H. Netzer, "L'extrême-onction aux VIII et IX siècles," *Revue du clergé français* 68 (1911), p. 202.
19. *Vita S. Berlendis* (PL 139:1108); *Vita S. Eugenii, Acta Sanctorum* 38, Aug. 23, p. 627; *Vita S. Hunnegundae*, in *Acta Sanctorum* 39; *Vita S. Tresani*, in *Acta Sanctorum* 5, Feb. 7, p. 55.
20. The *Vita S. Eugenii* was written in the ninth century, that of St. Cunegunda in the tenth, and the biography of St. Berlendus is attributed to the eleventh century.
21. Puller, *op. cit.*, p. 192; Ruch, *op. cit.*, col. 1962.
22. *Sacramentarium Gelasianum*, lib. 1, cap. 40 (PL 74:1099-1100; text also found in *Le Liber ordinum en usage dans l'Eglise wisigothique et mozarabe d'Espagne du $V^e$ au $XI^e$ siècle*, in *Monumenta Ecclesiae Liturgica* 5 (Paris, 1912), p. 23; E.A. Lowe, *The Bobbio Missal: A Gallican Mass-book* (London, 1920), pp. 172-173.
23. *Le Liber ordinum . . .*, in *Monumenta Ecclesiae Liturgica* 5, pp. 8-11.
24. Bede, *Expositio super Epistolas catholicas: In Epistolam S. Jacobi* (PL 93:39-40).
25. Caesarius of Arles (see n. 15), vol. 103, p. 225.
26. *Ibid.*, vol. 104, p. 751.
27. In Sermon 13 the Latin text reads: ". . . *oleum benedictum a presbyteris* humiliter ac fideliter petat, et inde corpusculum suum ungeat" (*ibid.*, vol. 103, pp. 66-67). In Sermon 52 the words are: ". . . *oleo benedicto a presbyteris deberent perungere*" (*ibid.*, vol. 103, p. 232).
28. See Netzer, *op. cit.*, p. 207; Doronzo, *op. cit.*, pp. 130-131.
29. Ruch, *op. cit.*, col. 1959; Bord, *op. cit.*, p. 111.
30. Chavasse, *op. cit.*, pp. 110-114; Boudinhon, *op. cit.*, pp. 401-402; Villien, *op. cit.*, pp. 642-643; Palmer, *op. cit.*, pp. 284-285; De Clercq, *op. cit.*, pp. 146-147.
31. The Latin text of *De rectitudine* (PL 40:1172-1173) reads: ". . . oleumque benedictum fideliter ab Ecclesia petat, unde corpus suum in nomine Christi *ungat.*"
32. De Sainte-Beuve, *op. cit.*, p. 53; Kern, *op. cit.*, pp. 16-17.
33. The Latin text of the *Emitte* (PL 74:1099-1100): "Emitte quaesumus, Domine, Spiritum sanctum paraclitum de coelis in hanc pinguedinem

olei quam de viridi ligno producere dignatus es ad refectionem mentis et corporis. Et tua sancta benedictio sit omni *ungenti, gustanti, tangenti* tutamentum corporis animae et spiritus ad evacuandos omnes dolores, omnem infirmitatem, omnem aegritudinem mentis et corporis." This same formula, somewhat modified, is found in the *Gregorian Sacramentary*. There only two modes are listed: ". . . ut tua sancta benedictione sit omni *ungenti, tangenti* tutamentum mentis et corporis" (H. Lietzmann, *Das Sacramentarium Gregorianum nach dem Aachener Urexemplar* [Münster, 1921], p. 5).
34. Both Ruch (*op. cit.*, col. 1965) and Porter (*op. cit.*, p. 83) are of the opinion that this ritual predates the eighth-century invasion of Spain by the Moors. H. Philippeau says it originates from the eighth century ("Extrême-onction," *Catholicisme hier, aujourd'hui, demain*, vol. 4 [Paris: Letouzey et Ané, 1956], col. 1009). The text is found in Férotin, *Le Liber ordinum . . .*, in *Monumenta Ecclesiae Liturgica* 5, pp. 71-73.

Chapter Four (pages 58-70)
---

1. Many authors, such as H. Netzer ("L'extrême-onction aux VIII et IX siècles," *Revue du clergé français* 68 [1911], p. 188), accept the traditional dating of the *Statutes*, while others, such as C. de Clercq ("Ordre, mariage, extrême-onction," *Bibliothèque catholique des sciences religieuses*, vol. 83 [1939], p. 137), question their authenticity. B. Poschmann (*Penance and Anointing*, trans. F. Courtney [New York: Herder and Herder, 1964], p. 242) is of the opinion that the *Statutes* come from sometime between the years 800 and 842. *Statuta*, PL 89:823.
2. Rabanus Maurus, *Commentarium in Matthaeum libri octi* (PL 107:892).
3. Haymo of Halberstadt, *Homiliae de tempore*, Homily 105 (PL 118:573).
4. Until recently it was generally held that the orders found in the *Capitular* originated from the time of Theodulf. More contemporary scholarship has convincingly challenged this dating. According to H. Porter, these rituals could not have been compiled until at least a century and a half after the death of Theodulf ("The Rites for the Dying in the Early Middle Ages, I: St. Theodulf of Orléans," *Journal of Theological Studies* 10 [1959], pp. 43-62). The text of the ritual can be found in E. Martène, *De antiquis Ecclesiae ritibus*, lib. 1, cap. 7, Order II; an inaccurate version is found in PL 105:207-208.

5. For the text of the Ambrosian ritual, see L. Muratori, *Antiquitates Italicae medii aevi* (Milan, 1741), t. 4, cols. 845-848.
6. For the text of the Greek *Euchologion*, see J. Goar, *Euchologion sive rituale Graecorum* (Graz: Akademische Druck- und Verlagsanstalt, 1960), pp. 332-346.
7. Texts may be found in F. Warren, ed., *Liturgy and Ritual of the Early Celtic Church* (Oxford: Clarendon Press, 1881), pp. 167-225.
8. The texts may be found in PL 78:524-526.
9. E. Martène, *De antiquis Ecclesiae ritibus*, vol. 1, lib. 1, cap. 7, art. 4. Reference is especially to Orders I, III, IV-VII, X-XVII.
10. "Order for the Visitation and Anointing of the Sick," in *The Leofric Missal*, ed. F. Warren (Oxford: Clarendon Press, 1883), pp. 238-241.
11. Egbert, *Poenitentiale*, lib. 1, pars altera, cap. 15 (PL 89:416).
12. *Ibid.*, cap. 2, cols. 411-412; cap. 3, cols. 412-413; cap. 10, col. 414.
13. Egbert, *Excerptiones e dictis et canonibus sanctorum Patrum concinnatae*, can. 21 (PL 89:382).
14. Halitgarius, *De poenitentiae*, lib. 3 (cap. 3, PL 105:677; cap. 10, PL 105:679; cap. 16, PL 105:680).
15. Hincmar, *Epistola ad omnes fideles*, no. 36 (PL 126:256).
16. Riculf, *Statuta*, no. 9 (PL 131:18); Regino, "De visitandis a presbytero infirmis," *De ecclesiasticis disciplinis et religione Christiana*, can. 105-118 (PL 132:214-215).
17. *Vita S. Adelhardi*, in *Acta Sanctorum* 1, Jan. 2, p. 109; *Vita S. Fulcrani*, p. 716; *Vita S. Roberti*, in *Acta Sanctorum* 6, Feb. 25, p. 615; *De vita et morte B. Virginis Maurae* (PL 115:1374); *Vita S. Chrothildis*, in *Monumenta Germaniae Historica, Scriptores rerum Merovingicarum*, vol. 2, p. 347.
18. H. Porter, "The Origin of the Medieval Rite for Anointing the Sick," *Journal of Theological Studies* 7 (1956), pp. 211-225.
19. *Liber sacramentorum* (PL 78:235).
20. Warren, *op. cit.*, pp. 171-173.
21. *Carolingian Order*, in *Liber sacramentorum* (PL 78:231-236); *Roman Order X* (PL 78:1020-1023); Martène *op. cit.*, lib. 1, cap. 7, Order I.
22. Goar, *op. cit.*, pp. 332-346.
23. Warren, *op. cit.*, pp. 167-171, 220-225.
24. Warren, *op. cit.*, pp. 238-241; Goar, *op. cit.*, pp. 332-346.
25. See the Latin order for anointing in the *Second Capitular*, the order in the *Sacramentary of Rheims*, that from the *Leofric Missal*, the *Roman Order X*, and *Orders IV, V, XII, XIV*, and *XV* as collected by Martène.
26. See the orders found in the *Second Capitular*, the *Book of Mulling*, the *Sacramentary of Rheims*, the *Codex Ratuldus*, the *Roman Order X*, and *Ordo III* of the Martène collection.

27. See the order from the *Leofric Missal* and *Orders IV, V, XII, XV* as collected by Martène.
28. *Codex Titianus* (PL 78:526-529).
29. *Carolingian Order*, in *Liber sacramentorum* (PL 78:236). See also the order from the *Codex Titianus*, *Order V, VII* of Martène, and that from the *Leofric Missal*.
30. *Sacramentary of Rheims* (PL 78:529-539).
31. Multiple celebrants are indicated in the orders from the *Sacramentary of Rheims*, the *Codex Titianus*, the *Leofric Missal*, and *Orders IV, V, VI, VII, XI, XIV*, and *XV* of Martène.
32. Goar, *op. cit.*, p. 338.
33. Egbert, *Poenitentiale* (PL 89:416).
34. Hincmar, *Capitula synodica data presbyteris*, cap. 10 (PL 125:779).
35. Christianus Druthmar, *Expositio in Evangelium Matthaei*, cap. 26 (PL 106:1343).
36. Note that the original Latin text of Innocent's letter reads: "Quod non est dubium de fidelibus aegrotantibus accipi vel intelligi debere, qui sancto oleo perungi possunt quod ab episcopo confectum non solum sacerdotibus, sed et etiam omnibus uti Christianis licet in sua aut in suorum necessitate *ungendum.*" Chrodegang, *Regula canonicorum* (PL 89:1088). Note that many commentators say that this text is not authentic. E. Doronzo (*De Extrema Unctione* [Milwaukee: Bruce Publishing Co., 1954], p. 122) says that it dates sometime after 817, and De Clercq ("Ordre, mariage, extrême-onction," p. 151) says that it is only in this later version that the text of Innocent's letter was reproduced.
37. Jonas of Orléans, *De institutione laicali*, lib. 3, cap. 14 (PL 106:261). Note Bede's *Commentaria in Epistolam S. Jacobi* (PL 93:39).
38. Halitgarius, *De poenitentia*, cap. 16 (PL 105:680). The text reads: "Qui sancto oleo perungi possunt, quod ab episcopo confectum non solum sacerdotibus sed omnibus utique Christianis in sua aut suorum necessitate ungendum."
39. This is the opinion held by Chavasse, Puller, De Letter, Murray, and, with some variations, Poschmann.

## Chapter Five (pages 71-87)

1. Pseudo-Abelard, *Epitome theologiae Christianae*, cap. 30 (PL 178:1744).
2. Hugh of St. Victor, *De sacramentis*, lib. 2, pars 15 (PL 176:577).
3. *Ibid.* (PL 176:578).
4. Hugh of St. Victor, *Summa sententiarum*, tract. 6, cap. 15 (PL 176:154).

5. Peter Lombard, *Liber IV sententiarum*, d. 23, *Libri sententiarum IV* (Florence: Ex typographicis Collegii S. Bonaventurae, 1916), p. 889.
6. *Ibid.*, d. 23, cap. 3, p. 890.
7. *Ibid.*, d. 23, cap. 4, p. 891.
8. Albert, *Commentaria in Librum IV sententiarum*, d. 23, a. 2, *Opera omnia*, vol. 30, p. 4.
9. *Ibid.*, a. 1, p. 3.
10. Thomas Aquinas, *Contra gentiles*, lib. 4, cap. 73, *Opera omnia*, vol. 12 (Paris: Vivès, 1874), p. 584.
11. Thomas Aquinas, *In quartum librum sententiarum*, d. 23, q. 2, a. 2, *Opera omnia*, vol. 11, p. 14.
12. *Ibid.*, q. 1, a. 2, p. 6.
13. *Ibid.*
14. *Contra gentiles*, p. 585.
15. Thomas Aquinas, *In quartum librum sententiarum*, d. 23, q. 2, a. 2, p. 15; Albert, *op. cit.*, a. 10, p. 17.
16. Thomas Aquinas, *ibid.*, a. 1, p. 12.
17. Thomas Aquinas, *Supplementum*, q. 31, a. 2, p. 12. One questions Thomas' argument here, given the longstanding tradition that the deacon is an ordinary minister of baptism, which sacrament gives grace.
18. Thomas Aquinas, *In quartum librum sententiarum*, q. 2, a. 3, p. 8.
19. Alexander of Hales, *Glossa in quattuor libros sententiarum*, vol. 4, d. 23 (Florence, Quarrachi, 1957), p. 387; Bonaventure, *In quartum librum sententiarum*, d. 23, a. 1, q. 1, in *Opera omnia*, vol. 66 (Paris: Vivès, 1882–1902), p. 134.
20. Alexander of Hales, *ibid.*, pp. 393–394; Bonaventure, *ibid.*, pp. 135, 143.
21. Alexander of Hales, *ibid.*, pp. 386–387.
22. Bonaventure, *op. cit.*, a. 2, q. 1, p. 142.
23. *Ibid.*, a. 1, q. 3, p. 139.
24. *Ibid.*
25. Gerald of Cambrai, *Gemma ecclesiastica*, vol. 2, cap. 4, *Rerum Britannicorum medii aevi scriptores*, vol. 21 (London: Longman, Green and Roberts, 1862), p. 13.
26. Gerald cites from Isidore, *Decretalia*, pars 3, d. 4, cap. 19.
27. Innocent V, *In quartum librum sententiarum commentaria*, d. 23, q. 2, a. 1 (Toulouse: A. Colomerium, 1651), pp. 253–254.
28. *Ibid.*, q. 1, a. 1, pp. 250–251.
29. Duns Scotus, *Quaestiones in librum quartum sententiarum*, d. 23, q. 1, *Opera omnia*, vol. 19 (Paris: Vivès, 1894), pp. 5–17.
30. Thomas Waldensis, *De sacramento Extremae Unctionis, De sacramentis*, cap. 163-164 (Venice: Typis Antonii Bassanensii, 1758), p. 942.

31. Simeon of Thessalonica, *De sacro ritu sancti olei*, cap. 285 (PG 155:518).
32. Synodus Exoniensis; see J. Hardouin, *Acta conciliorum et epistolae decretales, ac constitutiones Summorum Pontificum*, 12 vols. (Paris, 1714–15) 7:1080–81; Synodus Baocensis, can. 74: Hardouin, 8:1237; Odo de Soliaco, *Synodicae constitutiones*, cap. 7 (PL 212:62).
33. Odo de Soliaco, *ibid.; Constitutiones Ricardi Poore*, can. 67, 69: J. Hardouin, *op. cit.*, 7:107; Synodus Exoniensis, Hardouin, *op. cit.*, 7:1081.
34. Synodus Exoniensis, Hardouin, *ibid.*
35. *Synodicae constitutiones*, cap. 8, n. 3; *Constitutiones Ricardi Poore*, can. 68; *Constitutiones synodales Valentinae diocesis*, Hardouin, *op. cit.*, 8:1979; Synodus Exoniensis; Synodus Baocensis.
36. See, for example, Synodus Claromentensis, cap. 9: Hardouin, *op. cit.*, 7:337; Concilium Senonense: Mansi 32:1172.
37. Concilium Coloniense I (1536), Mansi 32, pp. 1268–69; Synodus Augustanus (1548), Mansi 32, p. 1316; Concilium Coloniense II (1549), Mansi 32, p. 1398.
38. See the profession of faith prescribed by Innocent III for the Waldensians (DS 794) and that for Michael Palaeologus issued by the Second Council of Lyons in 1274 (DS 860).
39. The principal orders referred to here as dating from this period include: *Ordo XVIII-XXX*, collected by E. Martène, *De antiquis Ecclesiae ritibus*, lib. 1, cap. 7, art. 4, pp. 917–956; three orders found in *Le Pontifical Romaine au moyen-âge*, ed. M. Andrieu, vol. 1-2 (Vatican City: Biblioteca Apostolica Vaticana, 1938, 1940): "Ordo ad ungendum infirmum," vol. 1, pp. 266–269; "Ordo visitationis infirmorum," vol. 1, pp. 270–277; "Ordo ad visitandum infirmum," vol. 2, pp. 486–495.
40. See *Ordo XXV* and *XXX* in Martène, *op. cit.*
41. Note those found in J. Goar, *Euchologion sive rituale Graecorum* (Graz: Akademische Druck- und Verlagsanstalt, 1960), and those collected by H. Denzinger, *Ritus Orientalium, Coptorum, Syriorum, et Armenorum*, vol. 2 (Würzburg: Stahelianis, 1864), especially: "Ritus ecclesiae Alexandrinae Copticorum ex rituali Gabrielis patriarchae," pp. 483–484; "Ordo lampadis Alexandrinus ex Tukio," pp. 484–501; "Ordo lampadis ex codicibus Vaticanis Copticism" pp. 501–506; "Ex codice Syriaco Vaticano," pp. 517–518; "Ex codice Armeno Bibliothecae Barberiniae Romae," pp. 519–523.
42. This is especially the case with the Armenian, Chaldean, Ethiopian, and Coptic Churches.
43. J. Launoy, *De sacramento unctionis infirmorum liber, Opera omnia*, vol. 1 (Coloniae Allobrogum, 1731). See especially: ex Pontificali Vien-

nense (c. 1500), pp. 502–506; ex *Manuale Lugdunense* (1548), pp. 507–509; ex *Manuale Suessionense* (1530), pp. 512–514; ex *Manuale Ambrianense* (1541), pp. 514–516; ex *Manuale Tullense* (1529), pp. 520–522; ex *Manuale Vindienense* (1554), pp. 522–525; ex *Manuale Metense* (1542), pp. 525–527; ex *Manuale Anciensi* (1527), pp. 527–530.

## Chapter Six (pages 88-102)

1. *The Geneva Confession*, trans. J.K.S. Reid, in *Calvin: Theological Treatises* (Philadelphia: Westminster Press, 1954), p. 26. It could be questioned whether in actual practice all the Reformers attributed such absolute authority to the Scriptures. Luther at times seems to have argued from tradition, as in his debate against Zwingli over infant baptism.
2. *Confessio Augustana* (1530), in *Melanthonis opera, Corpus Reformatorum* (hereafter CR), vol. 26, ed. H.E. Bindseil (Brunswick: C.A. Schwetschke, 1858), p. 279.
3. J. Calvin, *Institutio Christianae religionis* (1536), *Calvini: Opera omnia*, vol. 1, CR 29 (1863), p. 107.
4. P. Melancthon, *Apologia Confessionis Augustanae* (1530), *Melanthonis opera*, CR 27 (1859), p. 286.
5. Melancthon, *Repetitio Confessionis Augustanae sive Confessio doctrinae Saxonicarum Ecclesiarum ut Synodo Tridentinae exhiberetur* (1551), *Melanthonis opera*, CR 29, p. 1860.
6. Calvin, *Institutio Christianae religionis*, p. 952.
7. Melancthon, *Loci communes theologici* (1521), Library of Christian Classics 19, ed. W. Pauch (London: S.C.M. Press, 1955), p. 135.
8. Calvin, *Institutio Christianae religionis*, p. 1067.
9. M. Luther, *On the Babylonian Captivity of the Church*, trans. A.T.W. Steinhauser, in *Three Treatises* (Philadelphia: Muhlenberg Press, 1943), p. 126.
10. *Ibid.*, pp. 243–244. It should be noted that even though Luther understood penance principally as an opportunity for the sinner to call to mind the promise made at baptism, so that by placing one's faith in that promise one's sins would be forgiven, he continued to encourage the practice of confessing one's sins and receiving absolution as a good and pious practice. Luther, however, did not attribute the forgiveness of sins to the absolution but to the faith of the penitent who firmly believes that the words of the absolution are true.
11. Melancthon, *Prima adumbratio locorum theologicorum ab ipso auctore non edita*, in *Melanthonis opera*, CR 21 (1845), p. 43.

12. Melancthon, *Loci communes theologici*, p. 135.
13. Melancthon, *Apologia Confessionis Augustanae*, in *Melanthonis opera*, CR 28, pp. 286–287.
14. M. Bucer, *De regno Christi*, in *Melancthon and Bucer*, Library of Christian Classics 19 (1969), p. 240.
15. Calvin, *Institutio Christianae religionis*, p. 953.
16. Calvin, *De necessitate reformandae ecclesiae* (1543), *Calvini: Opera omnia* 6, CR 34, p. 487.
17. Calvin, *Institutes of the Christian Religion*, Book 4, ch. 28, Library of Christian Classics 21 (Philadelphia: Westminster Press, 1960), p. 1476.
18. Luther, *On the Babylonian Captivity of the Church*, in *Luther's Works* 36 (Philadelphia: Fortress Press, 1959), p. 116.
19. *Ibid.* Note also that Article 14 of the *Augsburg Confession* accepts that no one is to exercise the public offices of administering the Word and the sacraments in the Church unless called and commissioned by an act of the Church.
20. Luther, *Concerning the Ministry*, in *Luther's Works* 40, pp. 11–19.
21. *Ibid.*, p. 22.
22. *Ibid.*, p. 24.
23. *Ibid.*, p. 27.
24. *Ibid.*, p. 29. For the sense in which Luther was willing to accept the Mass as a sacrifice, see J. F. McCue, "Luther and Roman Catholicism on the Mass as Sacrifice," *Lutherans and Catholics in Dialogue* 3 (Washington: U.S.C.C. Publications Office, 1967), pp. 45–74.
25. *Ibid.*, p. 34.
26. Luther discusses the role of the community in appointing public ministers in *That a Christian Assembly or Congregation Has the Right and Power to Judge All Teaching and to Call, Appoint and Dismiss Teachers, Established and Proven by Scripture* (1523), in *Luther's Works* 39, pp. 305–314.
27. Luther, *On the Babylonian Captivity of the Church*, p. 237. Luther rejects the idea that the Epistle of James is the writing of any Apostle. First, it is contrary to Paul and all the rest of Scripture. James ascribes righteousness to works, which is contrary to Romans 4. Second, Luther notes that the purpose of the Epistle is to teach Christians, but it does not once mention the passion, resurrection, or Spirit of Christ. According to Luther, the duty of a true Apostle is to preach the passion, resurrection, and work of the Lord, and thus to lay the foundation of faith. This Epistle seems to speak more of the law and its work. Finally, the author of the Epistle wants to guard against those who rely on faith without works, and therefore, according to Luther, James insisted on the law to do what the Apostles accomplished by inciting

people to love (*Preface to the New Testament, Word and Sacrament* 1, in *Luther's Works* 35, pp. 395–398).
28. Luther, *On the Babylonian Captivity of the Church*, p. 237.
29. *Ibid.*
30. *Ibid.*, p. 238.
31. *Ibid.*, p. 239.
32. Luther, *Vom Abendmahl Christi Bekenntnis*, in *Luthers Werke* 26, p. 508.
33. Luther, *On the Babylonian Captivity of the Church*, pp. 241–242.
34. *Ibid.*, p. 241.
35. *Ibid.*, p. 239.
36. Melancthon, *Loci communes theologici* (see note 7), vol. 19, p. 136.
37. Melancthon further supported his position by noting that even the Church admits that extreme unction is not necessary for salvation (*Apologia Confessionis Augustanae*, CR 27 [1859], pp. 286–287).
38. Melancthon, *ibid.*, p. 570.
39. Melancthon, "De unctione," *Loci communes theologici*, (see note 7), vol. 21, p. 853.
40. Melancthon, *Repetitio Confessionis Augustanae, Melanthonis opera*, CR 28, p. 436.
41. Calvin, *Institutio Christianae religionis* (see note 3), p. 178.
42. *Ibid.*, pp. 142–143.
43. *Ibid.*, p. 179.
44. These Articles are reprinted in *A History of the Articles of Religion*, ed. C. Hardwick (London: F. and J. Revington, 1851), Appendix 1, pp. 231–248.
45. The *Bishops' Book* has been reprinted in *Formularies of the Faith*, ed. C. Lloyd (Oxford: University Press, 1825), pp. 21–211.
46. *Ibid.*, pp. 124–125.
47. The "Thirteen Articles of 1538" are reprinted in *A History of the Articles of Religion* (see note 44), Appendix 2, pp. 249–263.
48. *The King's Book*, intro. T. A. Lacey (London: S.P.C.K., 1932), pp. 78–82.

## Chapter Seven (pages 103–110)

1. N. Herborn, *Confutatio Lutheranismi Danici*, ed. B. Schmitt (Florence: Quaracchi, 1902), p. 154.
2. Herborn, *ibid.* See also J. Fisher, *Assertionis Lutheranae confutatio*, in *Opera omnia* (Würzburg: Apud Georgium Fleischmannum; republished London: Gregg Press, 1967), p. 331; J. Cochlaeus, *De gratia sacramentorum*, in *Johannis Cochlaei opuscula* (London: Gregg Press), p. 66.

3. Cochlaeus, *ibid.*
4. J. Fisher, *Contra Captivitatem Babylonicam Lutheri* (1523), in *Opera omnia*, p. 256.
5. Cochlaeus, *op cit.*, p. 67.
6. J. Eck, *Enchiridion locorum communium Joannis Eckii adversus Lutheranos* (Venice: Sabio, 1523), p. 21. See also B. Pirstinger, *Theologica Germanica* (1531), cap. 17, "De veritate verbali," nos. 2–3.
7. *Assertio septem sacramentorum*, ed. L. O'Donovan (New York: Benziger Bros., 1908), p. 402.
8. *Ibid.*
9. *Ibid.*, p. 356.
10. Pirstinger, *op. cit.*, cap. 17, no. 9.
11. Herborn, *op. cit.*, p. 159, regarding confirmation.
12. Eck, *op. cit.*, p. 29, regarding confirmation.
13. Pirstinger, *op. cit.*, cap. 57, "De sacramentis in genere," no. 11, regarding matrimony and penance.
14. *Ibid.*, no. 11, regarding confirmation, orders, and extreme unction.
15. *Ibid.*, cap. 93, "De extrema unctione," no. 2.
16. Herborn, *Locorum communium adversus huius temporis haereses enchiridion* (1529), ed. P. Schlager (Münster: Aschendorffische Verlagsbuchhandlung, 1927), p. 77.
17. *Assertio septem sacramentorum*, p. 440.
18. Cajetan, *In S. Marcum commentaria, Scripturae Sacrae cursus completus*, vol. 22, ed. J. P. Migne (Paris, 1842), p. 82.
19. Cajetan, *Epistolae Pauli et aliorum Apostolorum* (Paris: Apud J. Bodium Ascensium, J. Purvrum et J. Roigney, 1533), p. 212.
20. *Assertio septem sacramentorum*, p. 432.
21. *Ibid.*, p. 441.
22. Pirstinger, *op. cit.*, cap. 93, no. 4.
23. Eck, *op. cit.*, cap. 11, p. 38.
24. R. Tapper, *Explicationes articulorum venerandae facultatis sacrae theologiae generalis studii Lovaniensis*, vol. 1 (Louvain: M. Verhasselt, 1555), pp. 221–239.
25. P. DeSoto, *De institutione sacerdotum* (Venice: B. Rubinum, 1568), pp. 281–282.
26. Tapper, *op. cit.*, p. 227.

## Chapter Eight (pages 111-143)

1. *Concilium Tridentinum: Diariorum, Actorum, Epistularum, Tractatuum*, ed. Societas Goerresiana (Freiburg im Breisgau: Herder,

1964), vol. 5, p. 884 (hereafter referred to as CT). Note that both qualifications, "heretical" and "erroneous," seemed to merit anathematization.
2. The theologians referred to the Council of Florence, *Decretum pro Armenis,* from the bull "Exultate Deo" (DS 1310-1328); the Council of Constance, the bull "Inter cunctas" (DS 1151-1195), and *Interrogationes Wycliffitis et Hussitis proponendae* (DS 1247-1279). They also referred to the *Contra gentiles* and *In quartum librum sententiarum* of Thomas Aquinas and the *Sententiae* of Alexander of Hales.
3. This question was introduced by the Spanish Jesuit Diego Laynez, who suggested that an article be added that would state, "It is not a sacrament unless it is found in the Scriptures" (CT 5, p. 850).
4. In the Council's deliberations on the sacrament of confirmation, the second article submitted for investigation stated: "Confirmation was instituted by the Fathers and does not have the promise of the grace of God" (CT 5, p. 986). A variety of opinions were expressed regarding this article. Many felt that the article should be regarded as heretical and condemned. Others, admitting that the Church cannot institute a sacrament, qualified the mode of institution of confirmation by referring to Thomas Aquinas (*Suppl.*, q. 8, a. 1), who said that Christ instituted confirmation not by "exhibiting it" but by "promising it" (CT 5, p. 851). The Franciscan Andrea de Vega said outright that the testimony as to whether confirmation was instituted by the Apostles or by God is not clear (CT 5, p. 855).

In the canons promulgated on confirmation, there is no reference to the original article about confirmation being instituted by the Fathers nor an explicit reaffirmation that it was instituted by Christ. It can only be assumed that the Council was of the opinion that the institution of confirmation by Christ was to be understood by the general statement in canon 1 of the sacraments in general promulgated at the same session.
5. Francisco Herrera noted a verbal change in the form of baptism used by the Greeks which, he claimed, did not change the "substance of the sacraments" (CT 5, p. 853). Luis Carbaijal cited a change in the "form of confirmation" which in reality referred to a development of the matter of that sacrament (CT 5, p. 858).
6. Paulo Gregorianz, bishop of Zagreb, held that Communion under both kinds, even for the laity, is of divine law. He supported his opinion by noting that when Christ spoke his words in Matthew 26:27, they were not directed solely to the disciples. He also observed from Scripture that people received under both kinds (CT 7, p. 145). Georg Flach, bishop of Soli, referred to Paul ("As often as you drink . . .") and to Matthew 26:27 as a precept to be kept by all (CT 7, p. 156).

NOTES TO CHAPTER EIGHT (PAGES 111–143)     175

7. It was not until Session 21, more than ten years after Session 14, that Trent promulgated the mode of communicating the Eucharist. Again, the majority of bishops felt that Communion under both kinds was not of divine law and so could be changed by the Church. Opinions such as that of Amans of Brescia, a Servite theologian, continued to be expressed, namely, that even if it were a precept of Christ, the Church could change it.

    A number of bishops asked that a statement be included that would express that the Church has full power over the use and ritual of the sacraments. Thus in chapter 2 of the doctrinal chapters on the Eucharist, it was stated: ". . . this power has always been in the Church to establish or change those things in the dispensing of the sacraments, *salva illorum substantia . . .*" (CT 8, p. 690). Again, Trent did not explain what was meant by the phrase "the substance of the sacraments."
8. See Aurelio de Rocca (CT 5, p. 851); Nicolas Taborel (CT 5, p. 852); Giovanni Antonio Delfino (CT 5, p. 859).
9. It appears from the intervention of Mazochi that he was aware of the opinion that all Christians have that power without which there can be no sacrament, but they can exercise it only by the delegation of the Church or in the extreme circumstances that he describes as a "case of necessity" (CT 5, p. 860).
10. Gaspare Regis noted that the article was contrary to 1 Corinthians 14:13 (CT 5, p. 849). Girolamo Oleastro held that the article had already been condemned in canons 99 and 100 of the Fourth Council of Carthage and the Council of Florence (DS 1163). Sigismondo Fedrio cited the censure of the Council of Paris (1521), which rejected the position that all Christians, even priests, have equal power from God (CT 5, p. 863).
11. Mansi 3, p. 959.
12. "Errors of John Wycliff," no. 13 (DS 1163).
13. See Cornelio Musso (CT 5, p. 928); Baldassare Limpeo (CT 5, p. 988); Juan Fonseca (CT 5, p. 988); and Juan Salazar (CT 5, p. 939).
14. See Francisco de Navarra (CT 5, p. 989); Ambrogio Catarino (CT 5, p. 990).
15. Cardinal del Monte suggested that several bishops be sent to coax the absent Fathers to attend. There was general support for this suggestion. The Council would be restored to its full membership and give the impression that it was proceeding with its overall task. As Cornelio Musso, the bishop of Bitonto, stated, "The absent [should be] strongly forced to come to Bologna so that the Council not appear to be dissolved" (CT 6, p. 78).

16. Note the *Apologia Confessionis Augustanae*, art. 13, 6, *Melanthonis opera*, vol. 27, p. 570. See also CT 6, p. 96.
17. See *Vom Abendmahl Christi Bekenntnis*, in *Luthers Werke*, vol. 26, p. 508.
18. Two Augustinian theologians, Agostino Moreschini and Jeronimo of Salamanca, held that Mark 6:13 clearly demonstrates that extreme unction was instituted by Christ, for the Apostles only anointed at the mandate of Christ. Diego Laynez claimed that the Marcan text indicates that Christ instituted it "in some way." Richard of Le Mans and Thomas of Fogliano said that the passage shows that Christ "insinuated" the sacrament (CT 6, pp. 100-103, 112).
19. See the interventions made by Agostino Moreschini (CT 6, p. 102); Thomas of Fogliano (CT 6, p. 112); Thomas of Samarino (CT 6, p. 108); Jeronimo of Salamanca (CT 6, p. 114); Diego Laynez (CT 6, p. 103); Francisco Salazar (CT 6, p. 113); Julian of Colle (CT 6, p. 115).
20. See CT 6, pp. 102, 113-114.
21. See canon 34 of the Third Council of Carthage (Mansi 3:885D); canons 76-78 of the Fourth Council of Carthage (Mansi 3:957B); canons 47-48 of the Council of Laodicea (Mansi 2:571-572C).
22. Note the interventions of Richard of Le Mans (CT 6, p. 100); Jeronimo of Salamanca (CT 6, p. 114); Agostino Moreschini (CT 6, p. 102).
23. *De visitatione infirmorum* 2, 4 (PL 40:1154).
24. See Jeronimo of Salamanca (CT 6, p. 114); Pietro Januarius (CT 6, p. 100).
25. See Giovanni Antonio Delfino (CT 6, p. 102); Girolamo Bononi (CT 6, p. 103); and Cristoforo de Bagnacavallo (CT 6, p. 120), who all termed the first article "false," while Hercules Montuanus (CT 6, p. 99) and Delfino (CT 6, p. 102) held that the second article was "false."
26. See the interventions by Egidio Falcetta, Benedetto de' Nobili, and the bishops of Caprulanus and Aliphanus (CT 6, pp. 311, 315-316).
27. CT 6, p. 318. See also the interventions by Peter Vorstius (CT 6, p. 313); Aluigi Lippomano (CT 6, p. 314); and Cornelio Musso (CT 6, p. 315).
28. See the statements of the bishops of Sebenico (CT 6, p. 312), Motula (CT 6, p. 313), and Feltre (CT 6, p. 317).
29. See Benedetto de' Nobili (CT 6, p. 311); Cornelio Musso (CT 6, p. 315); and Sebastiano Pighino (CT 6, p. 316).
30. It should be recalled that Pope Innocent V, Hugh of St. Victor, and Richard of Middleton all seemed to be sympathetic to this theory to some degree.
31. See the interventions by Aluigi Lippomano (CT 6, p. 341) and Thomas Stella (CT 6, p. 342).

NOTES TO CHAPTER EIGHT (PAGES 111–143)

32. Note Ambrogio Catarino and Aluigi Lippomano (CT 6, pp. 342–343).
33. See Thomas Stella (CT 6, p. 353); Cornelio Musso (CT 6, p. 354); Benedetto de' Nobili (CT 6, p. 354); and Ambrogio Catarino (CT 6, p. 359).
34. Note the interventions by Tommaso Caselli and Ambrogio Catarino (CT 6, p. 353).
35. Regarding the sources noted for the other three articles, the *Acta* cite Luther's *Babylonian Captivity* and Melancthon's *Apologis* for article 1; Melancthon's *Loci communes* and *Apologia* and Calvin's *Institutes* for article 2. The same sources cited for the second article in 1547 are identified for article 3.
36. Johannes Arze and Rogerio Juvenis looked upon Mark 6:13 as establishing the sacramentality of extreme unction (CT 7, pp. 252, 259). Jodocus Ravesteyn admitted that at most the Marcan text prefigured the sacrament (CT 7, p. 256), and Sigismondo Fedrio saw extreme unction "foreshadowed" by the anointing in Mark (CT 7, p. 260).
37. Juvenis and Pietro Tagliavia see the text as establishing James' role as promulgator, and Fedrio, Ravesteyn, and Juvenis all saw in James 5:14-15 the elements necessary for a sacrament, thereby establishing the sacramentality of extreme unction (CT 7, pp. 256, 259–260, 286).
38. See Johannes Arze and Jodocus Ravesteyn (CT 7, pp. 252, 256).
39. There is no specific reference to the letter of Innocent I in Luther's writings. Calvin mentions it in chapter 19 of his *Institutes*.
40. The bishops of Palermo, Calahorra, Monopoli, and Salamis all asked that it be declared that extreme unction was "promulgated by James" (CT 7, pp. 328, 330–331).

# BIBLIOGRAPHY

Aubert, R. "Church History as an Indispensable Key to Interpreting the Decisions of the Magisterium." *Church History in Future Perspective.* Ed. R. Aubert. Concilium 57. New York: Herder and Herder, 1970, pp. 97–107.

Blenkinsopp, J. "Presbyter to Priest: Ministry in the Early Church." *Worship* 41 (Aug.–Sept. 1967), pp. 428–438.

Bord, J. B. *L'extrême-onction, d'après l'Epître de saint Jacques, Examinée dans la tradition.* Brussels: Beyaert, 1923.

Boudinhon, A. "La théologie de l'extrême onction." *Revue catholique des Eglises* 2 (1905), pp. 385–411.

———. "Si les fidèles se faisaient eux-mêmes autrefois les onctions de l'huile sainte." *Revue de clergé français* 68 (1911), pp. 722–728.

Bourke, M. "Reflections on Church Order in the New Testament." *Catholic Biblical Quarterly* 30 (1968), pp. 493–511.

Brown, R. *Priest and Bishop: Biblical Reflections.* New York: Paulist Press, 1970.

———. "Priestly Character: Sacramental Ordination." *Priest* 31 (1975), pp. 13–15.

Chaine, J. *L'Epître de Saint Jacques.* Paris: Gabalda, 1927.

Chavasse, A. *Etude sur l'onction des infirmes dans l'Eglise latine du $III^e$ au $XI^e$ siècle.* Lyons: Librairie du Sacré-Coeur, 1942.

———. "L'onction des infirmes dans l'Eglise latine du $III^e$ siècle à la réforme carolingienne. Les textes." *Revue des sciences religieuses* 20 (1940), pp. 290–364.

———. "L'onction des malades." *Manuel de dogme.* Paris: S. Sulpice, 1930.

Cleary, R. "Presbyterate in the Early Church." *Priest* 26 (May 1970), pp. 6–19.

Condon, K. "The Sacrament of Healing." *Scripture* 11 (1959), pp. 33–42.

Dauvillier, J. "Extrême-onction dans les Eglises orientales." *Dictionnaire de droit canonique* 5 (1951–52), pp. 725–789.

Davis, C. "The Anointing of the Sick." *The Furrow* 11 (Feb. 1960), pp. 75–80.

———. "The Sacrament of the Sick." *The Clergy Review* 43 (1958), pp. 726–746.

De Baets, M. "Quelle question le Concile de Trente a entendu trancher touchant l'institution des sacrements par le Christ." *Revue Thomiste* 14 (1906), pp. 31–47.

De Clercq, C. *Ordre, mariage, extrême-onction*. Bibliotheque catholique des sciences religieuses 83. Tours: Bloud et Gay, 1939.

De Guibert, P. "Extrême-onction." *Dictionnaire apologetique de la foi catholique* 1 (1911), pp. 1868–72.

De Letter, P. "Anathema." *New Catholic Encyclopedia* 1. New York: McGraw-Hill, 1967.

———. "The Meaning of Extreme Unction." *Theology Digest* (Autumn 1956), pp. 185–188.

De Sainte-Beuve, J. *Tractatus de sacramento Unctionis Infirmorum Extremae*, in Migne, *Theologiae cursus completus* 24. Paris: 1841, pp. 9–132.

Donovan, D. "Toward a Theology of the Ministry." *Homiletic and Pastoral Review* 70 (April 1970), pp. 489–499.

Doronzo, E. *De Extrema Unctione*. 2 vols. Milwaukee: Bruce, 1954–55.

Duval, A. "L'extrême onction au Concile de Trente." *La Maison-Dieu* 101 (1970), pp. 127–142.

Empereur, J. *Prophetic Anointing*. Message of the Sacraments 7. Wilmington, Del.: Michael Glazier, 1982.

Favre, R. "Les condamnations avec anathème." *Bulletin de littérature ecclesiastique* 47 (1946), pp. 233–238; 48 (1947), pp. 31–48.

Fransen, P. "The Authority of the Councils." *Problems of Authority*. Ed. J. Todd. Baltimore: Helicon Press, 1962.

———. "Réflexions sur l'anathème au Concile de Trente." *Ephemerides theologicae Lovanienses* 29 (1953), pp. 657–672.

Godefroy, L. "L'extrême onction chez les scholastiques." *Dictionnaire de théologie catholique* 5 (1913), cols. 1985–97.

Gusmer, C. *And You Visited Me: Sacramental Ministry to the Sick and the Dying*. New York: Pueblo Publishing Co., 1984.

"Issues of the Permanent Diaconate: Women and the Sacrament of the Sick." *Origins* 7 (March 16, 1978), p. 624.

Jacquemier, G. "L'extrême onction chez les Grecs." *Echos d'Orient* 2 (Oct. 1898–Oct. 1899), pp. 193–203.

Jedin, H. "Il Concilio di Trento—Scòpo, svolgimento e risultati." *Divinitas* 5 (1961), pp. 345–360.

Kasper, W. "A New Dogmatic Outlook on the Priestly Ministry." *The Ministry and Life of Priests Today*. Concilium 43. Ed. K. Rahner. New York: Herder and Herder, 1969, pp. 12–18.

# BIBLIOGRAPHY

Kern, J. *Tractatus dogmaticus de sacramento Extremae Unctionis.* Ratisbon: Pustet, 1907.
Kilmartin, E. "Office and Charism: Reflections on a New Study of Ministry." *Theological Studies* 38 (1977), pp. 547-554.
Koerperich, G. "De ministro Extremae Unctionis." *Collationes Namurcenses* 29 (1935), pp. 354-357.
Küng, H. *Why Priests?* Garden City, N.Y.: Doubleday, 1972.
Komonchak, J. "Church and Ministry." *The Jurist* 43 (1983), pp. 273-288.
Kuttner, S. "The Reform of the Church and the Council of Trent." *The Jurist* 22 (1962), pp. 123-142.
Lang, A. "Der Bedeutungswandel der Begriffe 'fides' und 'haeresis' und die dogmatische Wertung von Vienne und Trient." *Münchener Theologische Zeitschrift* 4 (1953), pp. 133-146.
Launoy, J. *De sacramento Unctionis Infirmorum liber, Opera omnia* 1. Paris, 1673; Coloniae Allobrogum, 1731.
Lawlor, F. X. "Heresy." *New Catholic Encyclopedia* 6. New York: McGraw-Hill, 1967, pp. 1062-63.
Leclercq, H. "Extrême-onction." *Dictionnaire d'archéologie chrétienne et de liturgie* 5 (1922), cols. 1029-37.
Lee, B. *The Becoming of the Church.* New York: Paulist Press, 1974.
Leff, G. *Heresy in the Later Middle Ages.* New York: Barnes and Noble, 1967.
Lennerz, H. "Notulae Tridentinae, Primum Anathema in Concilio Tridentino." *Gregorianum* 27 (1946), pp. 136-142.
Luff, S. "The Sacrament of the Sick: A First Century Text." *The Clergy Review* 52 (Jan. 1967), pp. 56-60.
McMorrow, K. "The Sacrament of the Anointing of the Sick: Historical-theological Considerations." *American Ecclesiastical Review* 169 (1975), pp. 507-521.
McSorley, H. "Luther, Trent, Vatican I and II." *McCormick Quarterly* 21 (Nov. 1967), pp. 95-104.
Michel, C. "Anathème." *Dictionnaire d'archéologie chrétienne et de liturgie,* vol. 1, part 2, col. 1932.
_____. "Hérésie." *Dictionnaire théologie catholique* 6 (1920), cols. 2211-58.
Mohler, J. *The Origin and Evolution of the Priesthood.* New York: Alba House, 1970.
Murray, P. "The Liturgical History of Extreme Unction." *The Furrow* 11 (1960), pp. 572-593.
Netzer, H. "L'extrême-onction aux VIII et IX siècles." *Revue du clergé français* 68 (1911), pp. 182-207.
Palmer, P. *The Doctrine on Penance and Extreme Unction.* Sources of Christian Theology 2. London: Darton, Longman and Todd, 1960, pp. 273-320.

_____. "The Purpose of Anointing the Sick: A Reappraisal." *Theological Studies* 19 (1958), pp. 309–344.

Peter, C. "Auricular Confession and the Council of Trent." *The Jurist* 28 (1968), pp. 280–297.

_____. "Integral Confession and the Council of Trent." *Sacramental Reconciliation*. Concilium 61. Ed. E. Schillebeeckx. New York: Herder and Herder, 1971, pp. 99–109.

Pickar, C. "The Epistle of James." *A Commentary on the New Testament*. Washington: The Catholic Biblical Association, 1942.

Porter, H. "The Origin of the Medieval Rite for Anointing the Sick." *Journal of Theological Studies* 7 (1956), pp. 211–225.

Poschmann, B. *Penance and Anointing of the Sick*. Trans. F. Courtney. New York: Herder and Herder, 1964.

Provost, J. "Toward a Renewed Canonical Understanding of Official Ministry." *The Jurist* 41 (1981), pp. 448–479.

Puller, F. *The Anointing of the Sick in Scripture and Tradition*. London: S.P.C.K., 1904.

Quesnell, Q. "From New Testament Text to Priesthood Tomorrow." *Chicago Studies* 10 (Summer 1971), pp. 187–200.

Rahner, K. *The Church and the Sacraments*. New York: Herder and Herder, 1963.

_____. *On Heresy*. New York: Herder and Herder, 1964.

_____. *The Priesthood*. New York: Herder and Herder, 1973.

_____. "Reflections on the Concept of *Ius Divinum* in Catholic Thought." *Theological Investigations* 5. Baltimore: Helicon Press, 1966, pp. 210–243.

_____. "What Is a Theological Starting Point for a Definition of the Priestly Ministry?" *The Ministry and Life of Priests Today*. Concilium 43. Ed. K. Rahner. New York: Herder and Herder, 1969, pp. 80–86.

_____. "What Is a Dogmatic Statement?" *Theological Investigations* 5. Baltimore: Helicon Press, 1966, pp. 45–90.

Ratzinger, J. *Priestly Ministry: A Search for Its Meaning*. New York: Sentinel Press, 1971.

Reiner, W. "Dogma and Heresy Revisited." *Thomist* 46 (1982), pp. 509–538.

Rouillard, P. "Le ministére du sacrement de l'onction des malades." *Nouvelle revue théologique* 111 (1979), pp. 395–402.

Ruch, C. "Extrême onction dans l'Ecriture." *Dictionnaire de théologie catholique* 5 (1913), cols. 1897–1927.

_____. "Extrême onction du I$^{er}$ au IX$^e$ siècle." *Dictionnaire de théologie catholique* 5 (1913), cols. 1927–85.

Schillebeeckx, E. "The Catholic Understanding of Office in the Church." *Theological Studies* 30 (1969), pp. 567–587.

———. *Christ the Sacrament of the Encounter with God.* New York: Sheed and Ward, 1963.

Schlier, H. "New Testament Elements of Priestly Office." *Theology Digest* 18 (1970), pp. 11–18.

Vacant, A. "Anathème." *Dictionnaire de théologie catholique* 1 (1903), cols. 1168-71.

Venard, M. "Le Concile de Trente: Aboutissement et point de départ." *Lumière* 33 (1984), pp. 49–56.

Verhamme, A. "De ministro Extremae Unctionis." *Collationes Brugenses* 45 (1949), pp. 186–199.

Villien, A. "L'extrême-onction." *Revue du clergé français* 70 (1912), pp. 640–667.

———. *Les sacrements, histoire et liturgie.* Paris: Gabalda, 1931.

JOHN J. ZIEGLER was ordained a priest of the Diocese of Syracuse, New York, in 1964. He obtained a bachelor of arts degree from St. Bernard's College, Rochester, New York (1961); a licentiate in theology from the Gregorian University, Rome (1965); and a doctorate in systematic theology from the Institute of Christian Thought of St. Michael's College, University of Toronto (1973). His doctoral research and dissertation focused on the Reformation/Tridentine period of Church history, with special attention to the question of extraordinary ministers of the sacrament of anointing.

In addition to pastoral ministry at St. Mary's of the Lake Parish in Skaneateles, New York, Father Ziegler has served as Director of Continuing Education, Director of the Permanent Diaconate, and Vicar for Planning and Research for the Diocese of Syracuse.